BEYOND BOUNDARIES:
MASTERING THE ART OF CRITICAL THINKING, REASONING & PROBLEM-SOLVING

ASTRAEA BACH

CONTENTS

INTRODUCTION

The capacity to think critically, argue persuasively and solve issues is more important than ever in today's complex and quickly changing world. These cognitive abilities are crucial to our success and well-being, whether managing personal relationships, making wise decisions, or succeeding at work. However, when looking through publications on this topic, many individuals who want to improve their critical thinking skills face several difficulties. These pain points, which range from a lack of practical application and complex terminology to a narrow domain focus and short engagement, can impede the learning process and restrict the use of learned abilities.

A book that goes beyond the limitations of conventional approaches to critical thinking, reasoning, and problem-solving is required in light of these difficulties. This book seeks to give readers insightful information, understandable language, specialized advice, interactive elements, and practical ideas for implementation in the real world. It offers a revolutionary learning experience that will empower individuals to master the skill of critical thinking and problem-solving, allowing them to traverse the complexities of life with assurance and clarity. By tackling these pain points head-on.

The author of this book is aware of the difficulties and constraints that readers may have encountered when trying to develop their critical thinking abilities. The author has created a solid profile by releasing other relevant publications in this field, ensuring credibility, and establishing knowledge. Readers can gain access to a comprehensive collection of resources that extensively explore the areas of consciousness, decision-making, logic, mental health, neuroscience, philosophy, psychology, and strategy by utilizing this expertise and grouping their works. The integrated approach increases the book's value, giving readers a comprehensive understanding of critical thinking, reasoning, and problem-solving.

Let's now examine the plethora of advantages readers stand to acquire from reading this book. It promises to improve critical thinking abilities first and foremost. Readers will embark on a trip that enhances and deepens their capacity to approach issues and circumstances with a more analytical and discriminating mentality by sifting through its pages.

They will gain knowledge of biases, how to assess material critically, and how to build compelling arguments. Readers will develop the ability to analyze complicated problems and draw sound, evidence-based conclusions through practical exercises and accessible examples.

Additionally, this book emphasizes the development of critical thinking skills. Readers will improve their reasoning ability and make informed decisions by engaging with its content. They will learn how to identify fallacies, evaluate the evidence, and put together strong arguments as they gain a greater understanding of the fundamentals of logical thinking. This improved capacity for review will benefit various spheres of life, from intimate connections and professional development to tackling societal issues and engaging in educated civic dialogue.

The emphasis on practical application is one of this book's defining qualities. Unlike many other resources that explain critical thinking and problem-solving in abstract terms, this book's ideas are grounded in relatable examples and practical activities. It acknowledges that the capacity to use intellectual abilities in practical contexts is the actual test of mastery. Readers can test their critical thinking, reasoning, and problem-solving skills through exciting activities and thought-provoking tasks. This practical, results-driven approach guarantees that readers gain theoretical comprehension and valuable expertise, translating into noticeable improvements in their daily lives.

Moreover, this book is written for readers from various fields and businesses, noting that how critical thinking abilities are applied varies depending on the situation. The book provides specialized advice for readers' interests, whether they are business executives, educators, or technologists. By addressing these domains ' distinct issues and scenarios, readers can learn domain-specific insights and tactics to improve their problem-solving and decision-making abilities. The book's content is adaptable, encouraging flexibility and equipping readers with the tools to solve challenges from various angles. The emphasis on practical application is one of this book's defining qualities.

The book follows five principles to produce valuable and exciting content: information, focus, organization, flow, and language. This will give readers practical and in-depth knowledge by exploring the nuances of reasoning, problem-solving, and critical thinking. Avoiding filler and pointless asides, the topic is conveyed briefly and directly to the point. The book's structure ensures that information is presented logically and coherently, enabling readers to traverse the subject matter quickly. The chapters and content flow well, making it easier for readers to understand and remember. Finally, the book's language is understandable and exciting, grabbing readers' attention and making learning fun.

Readers can anticipate a thorough and transforming journey with this book, providing them with the tools and techniques to master critical thinking, reasoning, and problem-solving. Readers can improve their analytical thinking, decision-making skills, and ability to confidently take on real-world situations more clearly and effectively by engaging with the content and the principles presented. The claims made in this book are supported by tested theories, solid research, and real-world examples, ensuring that readers have the skills necessary to flourish in a challenging and complicated world.

Finally, the time to use this book to start a revolutionary path of critical thinking, reasoning, and problem-solving. The demand for these invaluable skills continues to grow, and by seizing the opportunity to enhance cognitive prowess, readers will position themselves for success in every facet of life. Act immediately to improve your ability to think critically, make wiser choices, navigate challenges quickly, and realize your full potential. Those who can think critically and solve problems are on the road to a better future.

CHAPTER ONE
FOUNDATION OF CRITICAL THINKING

In this modern and intricate society we inhabit, where everything moves swiftly., critical thinking has become an essential skill for navigating through the myriad of information and challenges we encounter. This chapter will lay the groundwork for developing a solid foundation in critical thinking. We will look at the definition and significance of critical thinking, address the complexity and jargon often associated with the topic, and provide practical applications through real-life examples. By this chapter's end, you will understand what critical thinking entails and how it can enhance your problem-solving abilities. And exercises. By this chapter's end, you will understand what critical thinking entails and how it can improve your problem-solving skills.

Definition of Critical Thinking

Critical thinking encompasses a range of

cognitive skills and mental processes that enable individuals to approach information and problems systematically and analytically. It involves breaking down complex ideas or arguments into their constituent parts, examining the relationships between those parts, and assessing their strengths and weaknesses. By engaging in critical thinking, individuals can delve beneath the surface of information, uncover hidden assumptions, and evaluate the validity and reliability of evidence.

One of the key aspects of critical thinking is the ability to analyze information. This involves carefully examining the evidence, sources, and supporting arguments to assess their credibility and relevance. Critical thinkers consider the context in which information is presented and scrutinize the methodology used to gather or generate that information. They look for logical consistency, coherence, and internal contradictions within arguments, ensuring that conclusions are well-supported and grounded in sound reasoning.

Additionally, critical thinking involves evaluation, which requires individuals to assess the quality and value of different perspectives or viewpoints. Critical thinkers seek to understand the strengths and weaknesses of various arguments, recognizing that not all sources or opinions are equal in their credibility or reliability. They can discern between well-reasoned arguments and those based on faulty reasoning, bias, or insufficient evidence.

Synthesis is another essential component of critical thinking. They integrate different information or ideas to form a comprehensive understanding or generate new insights. Critical thinkers are adept at identifying connections, patterns, and relationships between disparate pieces of information, allowing them to develop a more nuanced and holistic perspective. By synthesizing information, critical thinkers can arrive at original and creative solutions to complex problems.

Furthermore, critical thinking encourages individuals to question assumptions and challenge conventional wisdom. It involves a willingness to explore alternative viewpoints and consider diverse perspectives, even if they differ from one's beliefs or preconceived notions. Critical thinkers recognize that intellectual growth and the pursuit of truth require an openness to new ideas, a willingness to reevaluate existing beliefs, and a commitment to intellectual humility.

Importance of Critical Thinking:
❖ Enhancing Problem-Solving Skills:

Critical thinking equips individuals with the ability to identify problems, analyze their underlying causes, and generate creative and effective solutions.

It enables individuals to approach complex issues systematically and analytically, leading to more innovative and well-reasoned outcomes.

❖ Decision-Making:

Critical thinkers can make informed decisions supported by evidence and logical reasoning by critically evaluating available information and considering different viewpoints. They are better equipped to weigh the pros and cons of various options, anticipate potential consequences, and select the most advantageous course of action.

❖ Fostering Open-Mindedness and Curiosity:

Critical thinking encourages individuals to challenge their beliefs, biases, and preconceived notions. It promotes an open-minded attitude that is receptive to new ideas, diverse perspectives, and alternative viewpoints. This intellectual curiosity fuels continuous learning and personal growth.

❖ Developing Strong Communication Skills:

Critical thinkers are adept at articulating their thoughts and ideas effectively verbally and in writing. They can construct coherent and logical arguments, present evidence to support their claims and engage in respectful and constructive discussions. These communication skills are invaluable in personal, academic, and professional contexts.

❖ **Navigating Information Overload:**
Critical thinking is crucial for navigating the vast data and sources available today's information-driven society. It helps individuals distinguish between reliable and biased information, evaluate the credibility of sources, and avoid falling prey to misinformation and manipulation.

❖ **Engaging in Ethical Decision-Making:**
Critical thinking is intertwined with ethical reasoning, enabling individuals to analyze ethical dilemmas, evaluate competing values and principles, and make moral judgments. It empowers individuals to consider the ethical implications of their actions and navigate complex moral landscapes.

Addressing Complexity and Jargon: Using Accessible Language and Clear Explanations

In mastering critical thinking, reasoning, and problem-solving, it is essential to address the challenges of complexity and jargon that often accompany these concepts. Critical thinking can be a complex subject, and using technical language and specialized terminology can create barriers for learners. To ensure effective communication and understanding, it is crucial to employ accessible language and provide clear explanations. By doing so, we can engage a wider audience and facilitate the learning process.

❖ **Simplifying Complex Ideas:**

When exploring intricate concepts related to critical thinking, it is essential to break them down into simpler, more digestible components. This involves distilling complex ideas into their fundamental elements and presenting them coherently and logically. By organizing information in a structured format, learners can better grasp the underlying principles and build a solid foundation for their understanding.

❖ **Clarifying Terminology and Definitions:**

Jargon and technical terminology can hinder the learning process, especially for individuals who are new to the subject. Therefore, defining and clarifying key terms and concepts throughout the learning materials is essential. By providing concise and easily understandable definitions, we can ensure that readers are on the same page and can follow the discussion without confusion. This approach allows learners to focus on comprehending the content rather than deciphering complex language.

❖ **Using Analogies and Real-Life Examples:**

Analogies and real-life examples are powerful tools for making complex ideas more relatable and understandable. By connecting abstract concepts to familiar situations, Metaphors aid in the transition from theory to implementation. Similarly, incorporating real-life examples and scenarios helps learners see the practical relevance of critical thinking in various contexts. These strategies enable individuals to grasp concepts more quickly and apply them to their lives.

❖ Visual Representations:

Graphical representations, including diagrams, charts, and information graphics, can enhance understanding by presenting information visually appealing and organized. Visual representations can simplify complex relationships and processes, making them more accessible to learners. Utilizing visual elements alongside clear explanations can aid in comprehending and retaining critical thinking concepts.

❖ Progressively Building Knowledge:

Adopting a step-by-step approach that progressively builds upon prior knowledge is crucial when introducing complex topics. This involves starting with foundational concepts and gradually introducing more progressive ideas. By structuring the learning material in a logical sequence, learners can develop a solid understanding of critical thinking without feeling overwhelmed by the complexity of the subject matter.

❖ Providing Context and Relevance:

To engage learners and emphasize the practical application of critical thinking, providing context and highlighting the relevance of the discussed concepts is essential. Exploring real-world examples, case studies, and applications of necessary thinking principles in different domains can demonstrate how these skills can be utilized in everyday life. By illustrating the benefits and practicality of critical thinking, learners are more likely to remain motivated and invested in the learning process.

❖ Encouraging Active Learning:

Engaging learners in active participation enhances their understanding and retention of complex concepts. Encourage readers to reflect on the material, ask questions, and participate in exercises and activities that require critical thinking. By actively involving learners, they become more invested in their learning journey and can better grasp complex ideas.

❖ Providing Contextualized Examples:

It is crucial to provide contextualized examples that illustrate how critical thinking is applied in different fields and situations to enhance understanding further. By presenting examples from diverse domains such as business, education, healthcare, or politics, readers can see the relevance and practicality of critical thinking in their areas of interest. These examples should be carefully selected to represent a range of scenarios, and Individuals may face problems in their personal and professional lives.

❖ Incorporating Interactive Elements:

Engaging readers in interactive elements, such as quizzes, case studies, and problem-solving exercises, can deepen their understanding of complex concepts. These interactive elements encourage readers to apply critical thinking skills in real-time and provide opportunities for self-assessment and reflection. By actively participating in these activities, readers can internalize the principles of critical thinking and develop their problem-solving abilities.

❖ Incorporating Multi-modal Learning:

People have diverse learning preferences, and incorporating multi-modal learning approaches can cater to different styles. Alongside written explanations, visual aids, audio or video content, and interactive online resources can help reinforce understanding. By appealing to various senses and learning styles, Learners can interact with the subject meaningfully, leading to a more comprehensive grasp of the subject matter.

❖ Addressing Common Misconceptions:

Critical thinking often involves challenging preconceived notions and biases. It is important to address common misconceptions and clarify any misunderstandings that may arise. By explicitly highlighting and debunking misconceptions, readers can overcome cognitive biases and better understand critical thinking concepts more accurately.

❖ **Encouraging Reflective Practice:**

The learning process cannot be complete without the crucial ingredient of reflection, particularly regarding critical thinking. Encourage readers to practice meditation by regularly pausing to review and evaluate their thinking processes. This self-assessment helps individuals identify areas for improvement, recognize cognitive biases, and refine their critical thinking skills over time.

Practical Application: Introducing Real-Life Examples and Exercises:

Theory alone is insufficient to develop mastery in critical thinking. Through practice and real-life application, we genuinely internalize the concepts and skills. In the upcoming segment, we shall provide diverse real-life examples demonstrating the application of critical thinking in different scenarios. These examples will cover various domains, such as personal relationships, professional settings, and societal issues. By examining these cases, you will gain insights into how critical thinking can be applied to solve problems, make informed decisions, and evaluate arguments effectively.

Engaging in practical applications and interactive exercises is essential for developing mastery of critical thinking. While theory provides the foundation and understanding of key concepts, it is through hands-on practice that we genuinely internalize and refine our necessary thinking skills. This section recognizes the importance of real-life applications and provides diverse examples and interactive exercises to enhance your learning experience.

Including real-life examples is crucial as it bridges the gap between theory and practice. You will better understand its practical application by investigating how critical thinking may be utilized in different disciplines, such as personal relationships, professional settings, and societal issues. These examples will present realistic scenarios requiring essential thinking skills to analyze, evaluate, and solve problems. Through examining these cases, you will witness firsthand the power and impact of critical thinking in everyday life.

Additionally, we have designed interactive exercises that encourage active engagement and application of critical thinking. These exercises are carefully crafted to challenge you to think critically, analyze information, and evaluate the validity of arguments. By actively participating in these exercises, you will sharpen your critical thinking abilities and develop the confidence to approach complex problems logically and systematically. These exercises will require you to consider different perspectives, weigh evidence, and make informed decisions based on careful reasoning.

We believe that providing practical exercises enhances your learning experience and makes the journey toward mastering critical thinking more enjoyable and fulfilling. Engaging in interactive activities allows you to actively Use the principles and abilities you've learned to give yourself a sense of accomplishment and improvement. It creates an environment that encourages curiosity, exploration, and intellectual stimulation.

Furthermore, the interactive nature of these exercises promotes self-reflection and self-assessment. As you tackle the challenges presented in these exercises, you will have the opportunity to reflect on your thinking processes, identify areas for improvement, and develop strategies to enhance your critical thinking skills. This reflective practice is invaluable as it allows continuous learning and refinement of your necessary thinking abilities.

We aim to provide a comprehensive, immersive learning experience by combining real-life examples and interactive exercises. Through practical application and active engagement, you will gain the knowledge and confidence to navigate challenging situations, make informed decisions, and effectively communicate your thoughts and ideas. We invite you to embrace these opportunities for growth and challenge yourself to think critically in various contexts.

TAKEAWAY

In this opening chapter, we have laid the foundation for your journey toward mastering the art of critical thinking. We have explored the definition and importance of critical thinking, ensuring the concept is accessible to all readers by addressing complexity and jargon. Additionally, we have provided practical applications through real-life examples and engaging exercises, allowing you to apply critical thinking skills in various contexts.

As you proceed to the subsequent chapters, you will delve deeper into the intricacies of critical thinking, reasoning, and problem-solving. Each chapter will build upon the knowledge and skills acquired in the previous chapters, offering you a comprehensive framework to develop your critical thinking abilities. Upon finishing this book, you will possess the essential skillset and approach needed to face obstacles confidently, assess data systematically, and arrive at intelligent judgments. Now, let us move forward to Chapter 2, where we will explore the development of a critical mindset and strategies for overcoming common barriers to critical thinking. Become ready for an exhilarating adventure that will enable you to surpass limitations and unleash the genuine capabilities of your cognitive abilities.

CHAPTER TWO
DEVELOPING A CRITICAL MINDSET

Overcoming Common Barriers to Critical Thinking

The Influence of Assumptions and Preconceived Notions:

One of the primary barriers to critical thinking is the tendency to rely on assumptions and preconceived notions. Our beliefs and biases can shape our interpretation of information and influence our decision-making process. To overcome this barrier, we must first develop an awareness of our assumptions and be willing to challenge them. By questioning the validity of our beliefs and seeking evidence to support or refute them, we can open ourselves to new perspectives and possibilities.

❖ Confirmation Bias:

Confirmation bias is another significant barrier that prevents us from thinking critically. It refers to our tendency to seek out and interpret information confirming our beliefs while disregarding or downplaying contradictory evidence. Overcoming confirmation bias requires a deliberate effort to expose ourselves to diverse viewpoints and alternative sources of information. By actively seeking out conflicting perspectives and engaging in thoughtful analysis, we can mitigate the influence of confirmation bias and arrive at more well-rounded conclusions.

❖ Emotional Biases:

Emotions have a substantial impact on our decision-making and can hinder critical thinking. Emotional biases can cloud our judgment and lead us to make irrational or impulsive decisions. One cognitive bias is the availability heuristic, which involves using readily available examples when assessing a situation or forming an opinion. Our tendency to recall or imagine vivid examples may cause us to perceive the probability of particular occurrences inaccurately. To conquer subjective attitudes based on emotions, we must strive to cultivate emotional intelligence and self-regulation. By developing an awareness of our feelings and their potential impact on our thinking, we can detach ourselves emotionally from a situation and approach it with greater objectivity. Taking the time to reflect and analyze the underlying reasons for our emotional reactions can help us make more reasoned and rational decisions.

❖ Cultural and Societal Influences:

Our beliefs and perspectives are often shaped by the society in which we live, and these influences can restrict our ability to think critically and question the status quo. Social conformity is when individuals adjust their beliefs and behaviours to align with a larger group. This can hinder independent thinking and discourage the exploration of alternative viewpoints. To overcome societal influences, we must cultivate a sense of intellectual independence and develop the courage to challenge prevailing norms and assumptions. This requires a willingness to question authority, debate respectfully, and seek diverse perspectives. We can broaden our understanding and develop a more nuanced and critical view by actively seeking information and viewpoints that challenge our own.

❖ Lack of Information Literacy:

In the era of abundant information, a lack of information literacy can pose a significant barrier to critical thinking. Information literacy involves locating, evaluating, and effectively using data from various sources. Without these skills, we may struggle to discern credible information from misinformation or propaganda. To overcome this barrier, it is essential to develop information literacy skills, including assessing the reliability and credibility of sources, critically analyzing information for bias, and distinguishing between fact and opinion. By honing our information literacy skills, we can confidently navigate the vast sea of information and make informed decisions based on reliable evidence.

❖ Limited Perspective and Narrow Thinking:

Another common barrier to critical thinking is limited perspective and narrow thinking. This occurs when we become entrenched in our worldview, failing to consider alternative viewpoints and possibilities. To overcome this barrier, it is crucial to cultivate a growth mindset and embrace a willingness to explore diverse perspectives. Actively seeking out different viewpoints, engaging in constructive debates, and exposing ourselves to new experiences can help broaden our thinking and challenge our beliefs. By embracing intellectual humility and recognizing that our perspective is just one among many, we can develop a more comprehensive and open-minded approach to critical thinking.

❖ Lack of Intellectual Curiosity:

Intellectual curiosity is a driving force behind critical thinking. It fuels our desire to seek knowledge, ask questions, and explore new ideas. However, a lack of intellectual curiosity can hinder our ability to think critically. To overcome this barrier, it is essential to cultivate a sense of wonder and curiosity about the world around us. We can engage in activities stimulating our intellectual curiosity, such as reading diverse books, attending thought-provoking lectures, or engaging in meaningful conversations with people from different backgrounds. By fostering intellectual curiosity, we unlock a world of learning opportunities and expand our capacity for critical thinking.

❖ Fear of Failure or Making Mistakes:

Fear of failure or making mistakes can significantly impede critical thinking. We may avoid taking risks or exploring unconventional solutions when we fear being wrong or making errors. Acknowledging that setbacks and mistakes are vital in personal development and gaining knowledge is crucial. Smartly overcoming this obstacle necessitates cultivating resilience and adopting a growth-oriented mentality. If we can change our perception of failure from a negative outcome to a chance for improvement and education, we can conquer our apprehension towards committing errors. Embracing a willingness to experiment, learn from setbacks, and adapt our thinking based on new insights enables us to approach problems with a more innovative and critical mindset.

❖ Time Constraints and Impatience:

Time constraints and impatience hinder our

critical thinking ability in our fast-paced world. When pressured to make quick decisions or find immediate solutions, we may rely on shortcuts or make hasty judgments without thorough analysis. Overcoming this barrier requires cultivating patience and recognizing the value of taking the time to think critically. It involves setting aside time for reflection and analysis, breaking complex problems into manageable parts, and engaging in systematic and thorough reasoning. By prioritizing the quality of our thinking over speed, we can overcome the limitations imposed by time constraints and make more informed and thoughtful decisions.

❖ Lack of Self-Reflection and Metacognition:

Critical thinking involves analyzing external information and reflecting on our thinking processes. However, a lack of self-reflection and metacognition can hinder our critical thinking ability. Developing self-awareness and engaging in metacognitive practices is essential to overcome this barrier. This involves regularly reflecting on our thinking, examining our biases and assumptions, and evaluating the effectiveness of our problem-solving strategies. By actively monitoring and adjusting our thinking processes, we can enhance our critical thinking skills and identify areas for improvement.

Encouraging Curiosity and Open-Mindedness

The Significance of Curiosity:

Curiosity is the driving force behind intellectual growth and discovery. It compels us to seek knowledge, question the world, and continuously expand our understanding. Curiosity sparks our interest, ignites our passion for learning, and propels us to explore diverse subjects and ideas. By embracing curiosity, we open doors to new possibilities and uncover hidden insights to enhance our critical thinking abilities.

Curiosity and Critical Thinking:

Curiosity and critical thinking go hand in hand. A curious mindset encourages us to investigate critically, examine the evidence, and evaluate information. It prompts us to ask probing questions, challenge assumptions, and seek multiple perspectives. Curiosity fuels our desire to dig deeper, uncover underlying causes, and arrive at well-reasoned conclusions. We unlock a robust intellectual growth and problem-solving tool by integrating interest into our critical thinking process.

The Role of Open-Mindedness:

Open-mindedness is the willingness to consider and accept new ideas, perspectives, and information, even if they challenge our existing beliefs. It is the antidote to cognitive biases and the key to expanding our thinking beyond preconceived notions. Open-mindedness allows us to approach discussions and debates with empathy, actively listen to diverse viewpoints, and engage in constructive dialogue. By embracing open-mindedness, we create an environment conducive to critical thinking and collaborative problem-solving.

Strategies to Foster Curiosity and Open-Mindedness:

- **Embrace a Growth Mindset:** Adopting a growth mindset, as coined by psychologist Carol Dweck, involves believing in the potential for growth and improvement. By understanding that our abilities and intelligence can be developed through effort and perseverance, we cultivate a curiosity-driven mindset that welcomes challenges and values the learning process. (Dweck, 2006)

- **Ask Thought - Provoking Questions:** Curiosity thrives on questioning. Encourage yourself to ask thought-provoking questions about the world, societal issues, and your beliefs. Engage in self-reflection and introspection to challenge assumptions and deepen your understanding of various topics.

- **Seek Diverse Perspectives:** Seek diverse perspectives from different cultures, backgrounds, and disciplines. Engage in conversations, read books from various authors, and explore alternative viewpoints.

Exposing yourself to diverse ideas fosters open-mindedness, broadens your thinking, and helps you see issues from multiple angles.

- **Practice Active Listening:** When engaging in conversations or debates, practice active listening. Give others your full attention, seek to understand their perspectives, and genuinely consider their points of view. Active listening promotes empathy, fosters respect, and creates a conducive environment for open-mindedness and critical thinking.

- **Embrace Discomfort:** Open-mindedness often requires stepping outside of our comfort zones. Challenge yourself to explore ideas that may initially feel uncomfortable or unfamiliar. Engaging with different perspectives and confronting cognitive dissonance enables growth and expands your critical thinking abilities.

- **Cultivate Intellectual Humility:** Recognize that you don't have all the answers and that there is always more to learn. Cultivating intellectual humility involves acknowledging gaps in your knowledge, being open to correction, and valuing the insights and expertise of others. This mindset fosters curiosity, encourages collaboration, and enhances critical thinking.

Interactive Exercises: Challenging Assumptions and Biases

To cultivate a discerning perspective, engaging in interactive activities that question our preconceptions and prejudices can be exceedingly fruitful. In this section, we will provide a series of engaging exercises designed to help readers recognize and overcome their preconceived notions. These exercises will involve analyzing thought-provoking scenarios, engaging in debates, conducting self-reflection, and practising empathy. By actively participating in these exercises, readers will gain a deeper understanding of their biases, develop the ability to think critically from multiple perspectives and enhance their problem-solving skills.

Exercise 1: The Assumption Challenge

Assumptions can limit our thinking and prevent us from considering alternative viewpoints or exploring new possibilities. This exercise challenges readers to identify and examine their assumptions by analyzing a given scenario.

- **Step 1:** Choose a scenario: Select a design from a list or create one yourself. The system should involve a situation where assumptions play a significant role. For example, "A new employee joins a team, and some team members assume they won't contribute much because of their age."

- **Step 2:** Identify assumptions: List the premises in the scenario. Encourage readers to think critically about the underlying beliefs and biases that drive these assumptions. For example, deductions might include "Younger employees lack experience" or "Older employees are resistant to change."

- **Step 3:** Challenge the assumptions: Prompt readers to question the validity of each hypothesis. Please encourage them to consider counterexamples, seek additional information, or explore alternative perspectives. This process helps readers recognize the limitations of their beliefs and broadens their thinking.

- **Step 4:** Reflect and evaluate: Readers should reflect on their findings after challenging the assumptions. Did their perspective change? Did they gain new insights or perspectives? Encourage readers to document their reflections and discuss their experiences with others to foster a collaborative learning environment.

Exercise 2: The Bias Exploration

Biases can significantly impact our critical thinking and decision-making processes. This exercise aims to help readers identify their preferences, understand their origins, and develop strategies to mitigate their influence.

- **Step 1:** Identify common biases: Introduce readers to cognitive biases such as confirmation, availability, or anchoring biases. Explain each tendency and provide examples to illustrate how they affect our thinking.
- **Step 2:** Self-reflection: Encourage readers to reflect on their own biases. Ask them to consider situations where they may have fallen prey to cognitive biases in the past. By analyzing personal experiences, readers can become more aware of their preferences and their impact on decision-making.
- **Step 3:** Case studies: Provide readers with case studies or real-life examples highlighting biases' influence. Ask them to identify the preferences in each case and discuss the potential consequences of those biases. This exercise helps readers apply their knowledge of tendencies in practical scenarios.
- **Step 4:** Mitigation strategies: Guide readers in exploring strategies to mitigate biases. Discuss techniques such as seeking diverse perspectives, self-reflection, fact-checking, and considering evidence from multiple

sources. Encourage readers to develop strategies that align with their learning styles and preferences.

Exercise 3: Empathy and Perspective-Taking

Empathy is crucial in critical thinking, enabling us to understand and appreciate diverse perspectives. This exercise focuses on developing empathy and practicing perspective-taking to enhance problem-solving abilities.

- **Step 1:** Present conflicting perspectives: Provide readers with a scenario or a topic that elicits diverse opinions. It could be a current social issue, a moral dilemma, or a complex problem. Present different perspectives and arguments related to the scenario.
- **Step 2:** Analyze and understand perspectives: Prompt readers to analyze each perspective and try to understand the underlying values, beliefs, and experiences that shape them. Please encourage them to suspend judgment and genuinely consider the validity of each viewpoint.
- **Step 3:** Engage in debates or discussions: Organize group discussions or debates where readers can share and defend different perspectives. Encourage respectful dialogue and active listening. This exercise fosters critical thinking by challenging readers to

articulate and defend their views while being open to alternative viewpoints.

- **Step 4:** Reflect and evaluate: Ask readers to reflect on their experience after the discussions or debates. Did they gain a deeper understanding of the topic? Did their perspective change? Please encourage them to consider the impact of empathy and perspective-taking on their critical thinking skills.

TAKEAWAY

In this chapter, we have explored the crucial process of developing a critical mindset. By overcoming common barriers to critical thinking, fostering curiosity and open-mindedness, and engaging in interactive exercises that challenge assumptions and biases, readers can cultivate the foundation for practical critical thinking. Developing a crucial mindset allows individuals to approach problems and situations with clarity, objectivity, and a willingness to consider diverse perspectives. By embracing a refreshing attitude, readers can unlock their full potential in mastering the art of critical thinking, reasoning, and problem-solving.

We will build upon the critical mindset developed here as we continue our journey in the following chapters. We'll explore the fundamental concepts of rational thinking, explore problem-solving strategies, analyze information, foster creativity and innovation, enhance collaboration and communication skills, address ethical considerations, and adapt to uncertainty and change. Each chapter will provide valuable insights, practical exercises, and real-life examples to further strengthen your critical thinking skills.

It is essential to remember that developing critical thinking skills is ongoing. As you progress through the upcoming chapters, I encourage you to engage with the content actively, reflect on your thinking processes, and apply the strategies and techniques to various aspects of your life. Challenge yourself to seek out diverse perspectives, question assumptions, and approach problems with a critical and analytical mindset.

By continuing this journey and investing in your growth as a critical thinker, you will gain invaluable skills that extend far beyond the pages of this book. Critical thinking will become an automatic component of your mental processes, empowering you to make well-informed decisions, navigate complex situations, and contribute meaningfully to your personal and professional endeavours.

So, let us proceed to the next chapter with excitement and determination. The path to mastering the art of critical thinking, reasoning, and problem-solving awaits, and I am confident that you have the potential to become an exceptional critical thinker.

Together, let us go beyond boundaries and unlock the transformative power of critical thinking.

CHAPTER THREE
THE POWER OF REASONING

Understanding the Principles of Logical Reasoning

Logical reasoning is a fundamental aspect of critical thinking that allows us to analyze and evaluate information, draw valid conclusions, and make informed decisions. By understanding the principles of logical reasoning, we can navigate complex problems, engage in effective communication, and challenge faulty arguments. This section will explore the critical components of logical reasoning and provide practical examples to illustrate their application in everyday situations.

One of the essential aspects of logical reasoning is deductive reasoning. Deductive reasoning involves drawing specific conclusions based on general principles or premises. It follows a top-down approach, starting with public statements and narrowing down to specific findings. The structure of deductive arguments relies on syllogisms, which consist of a central premise, a minor premise, and a conclusion. Let's consider an example:

Central Premise: All mammals are warm-blooded.
Minor Premise: Dogs are mammals.
Conclusion: Therefore, dogs are warm-blooded.

This example shows how the central premise establishes a general principle about mammals being warm-blooded. The minor premise then provides a specific example of a mammal, which is a dog. By applying deductive reasoning, we can logically conclude that dogs are warm-blooded.

Another critical aspect of logical reasoning is categorical logic, which involves sense based on categories and relationships between them. Categorical logic utilizes statements concerning classes or types, and their relationships, such as inclusion or exclusion. Let's consider the following example:

Statement 1: All birds have feathers.
Statement 2: Penguins are birds.
Conclusion: Therefore, penguins have feathers.

In this example, we have two categorical statements. The first statement establishes a general principle about birds having feathers. The second statement provides a specific example of a bird, which is a penguin. We can conclude that penguins have feathers based on their bird classification by applying categorical logic.

Understanding the principles of logical reasoning permits us to assess the legitimacy and strength of arguments. It helps us identify logical fallacies and reasoning errors undermining an argument's credibility. Logical fallacies, such as ad hominem attacks, straw man arguments, or false dichotomies, can manifest in various forms. By familiarizing ourselves with these fallacies, we can critically evaluate ideas and avoid being misled by faulty reasoning.

To further enhance our understanding of logical reasoning, it is essential to engage in practical application. By applying logical reasoning to everyday situations, we can develop our skills and become more adept at reasoned judgments. This involves actively seeking out and analyzing arguments, assessing their premises and conclusions, and considering alternative perspectives. Practising logical reasoning can refine our critical thinking abilities and strengthen our capacity to engage in thoughtful discussions.

Practical Application: Applying Logical Reasoning to Everyday Situations

Logical reasoning is not confined to academic or philosophical realms; it plays a crucial role in our everyday lives. Whether making decisions, evaluating information, or solving problems, logical reasoning provides a systematic approach to navigating the complexities of the world around us. This section will explore the practical application of logical reasoning to everyday situations, equipping readers with the skills to think critically and make informed choices.

One common area where logical reasoning is relevant is in evaluating advertisements. In the present-day society that prioritizes consumerism, we are constantly exposed to ads that advertise a wide range of products and services. One must cultivate the skill of analyzing messages critically to make wise choices when purchasing goods. Logical reasoning allows us to assess the claims made in advertisements and consider the evidence provided to support those claims. We can distinguish between valid arguments and manipulative tactics by applying logical principles such as sound reasoning and evidence-based evaluation. Through interactive exercises, readers will be guided to deconstruct advertisements, identify logical fallacies, and recognize when an idea lacks sufficient evidence.

Another aspect of everyday life where logical reasoning is invaluable is assessing news articles and information sources. In the digital age, we are inundated with a vast amount of information, making it crucial to have the skills to evaluate the credibility and reliability of sources critically. Logical reasoning helps us separate factual information from misinformation or biased content. By examining the arguments presented in news articles and considering the evidence and logical coherence, we can determine the credibility of the information. We will explore techniques for fact-checking, identifying logical inconsistencies, and recognizing discriminatory language. Readers will learn how to navigate the information landscape and make well-informed judgments through engaging examples and exercises.

Logical reasoning also plays a significant role in problem-solving, which is an essential skill in our daily lives. From simple challenges to complex issues, logical reasoning allows us to break down problems, identify underlying causes, and develop practical solutions. We can analyze the available information using deductive and inductive reasoning, make logical inferences, and conclude. We will explore problem-solving frameworks such as the scientific method, root cause analysis, and design thinking, which provide structured approaches to addressing problems. Through interactive exercises, readers can apply these problem-solving strategies to real-life scenarios, honing their logical reasoning skills and enhancing their problem-solving abilities. (Dowden, 1993)

One area where logical reasoning is particularly relevant is in personal relationships and communication. Interactions with family, friends, and colleagues often involve differing opinions, conflicting interests, and complex dynamics. We can analyze arguments, identify underlying assumptions, and construct logical responses using logical reasoning. This enhances our ability to engage in constructive and meaningful conversations, resolve conflicts, and maintain healthy relationships. Logical reasoning helps us navigate disagreements by focusing on the merits of the arguments rather than engaging in fallacies or emotional sense.

Another practical application of logical reasoning is evaluating the validity of scientific claims and research findings. In a world where scientific information is constantly being generated and disseminated, evaluating scientific claims critically is crucial. Logical reasoning enables us to assess the strength of scientific evidence, identify logical fallacies or biases in research studies, and distinguish between correlation and causation. By engaging in logical analysis, we can make informed judgments about scientific claims and contribute to evidence-based decision-making in various fields, such as healthcare, environmental issues, and public policy.

Furthermore, logical reasoning can assist us in

making sound decisions amidst uncertainty. Life is filled with situations where we must weigh the pros and cons, consider various options, and assess potential outcomes. Logical reasoning provides decision-making frameworks such as cost-benefit analysis and decision trees, which help us evaluate the advantages and disadvantages of different choices. By employing logical thinking, we can assess the probability and impact of different outcomes, enabling us to make informed decisions. Through practical exercises, readers can apply these decision-making tools to everyday dilemmas, strengthening their ability to think critically and make reasoned choices.

Specialized Reasoning Techniques for Specific Domains

In our exploration of critical thinking and reasoning, we have come to understand that reasoning skills vary across different domains. Applying logical reasoning effectively in specific fields can greatly enhance problem-solving and decision-making. This section will delve into specialized reasoning techniques tailored to exact domains, such as business, education, and other professional areas. By understanding the unique challenges and contexts faced in each field, we can develop a deeper appreciation for the relevance and application of logical reasoning.

Business and Management

Reasoning in the business and management domain requires a strategic and analytical approach. From strategic planning and financial analysis to decision-making under uncertainty, applying logical reasoning plays a pivotal role. Let's explore some specialized reasoning techniques that can empower professionals in the business world.

SWOT analysis (Strengths, Weaknesses, Opportunities, and Threats) is essential in business reasoning. SWOT analysis allows us to assess the internal and external factors affecting an organization, enabling informed decision-making and strategy development. By systematically evaluating strengths, weaknesses, opportunities, and threats, businesses can capitalize on their advantages, address weaknesses, seize opportunities, and mitigate threats.

Another valuable tool is cost-effectiveness analysis. This technique evaluates alternatives based on their costs and expected benefits to determine the most efficient and effective action. By applying logical reasoning to weigh the costs and benefits of various options, businesses can optimize resource allocation and maximize outcomes.

Additionally, game theory provides a framework for strategic decision-making in competitive situations. By applying logical reasoning to analyze the actions and interactions of multiple parties, businesses can anticipate and respond strategically to the behaviour of competitors, suppliers, and customers. Game theory helps companies to make informed decisions in complex and uncertain scenarios.

This chapter will present practical examples and exercises that illustrate applying specialized reasoning techniques in the business and management domain. By engaging with these examples, readers will understand how logical reasoning can enhance decision-making, strategic planning, and business problem-solving.

Education and Pedagogy

Reasoning skills are essential for educators and learners alike. In education, critical thinking and logical reasoning are crucial for curriculum design, classroom instruction, and fostering student engagement. Let's explore some specialized reasoning techniques that can enhance educational practices.

Curriculum design requires thoughtful reasoning to ensure learning objectives align with students' needs and educational goals. Educators employ logical reasoning to determine the sequencing of topics, select appropriate instructional strategies, and design assessments that accurately measure student learning. Educators can create cohesive and compelling learning experiences by applying logical reasoning to curriculum design.

Promoting critical thinking in the classroom is another vital aspect of education. Educators employ specialized reasoning techniques to develop students' analytical and problem-solving abilities. They encourage students to evaluate evidence, analyze arguments, and draw logical conclusions. Educators foster a critical thinking and reasoning culture by engaging students in activities that challenge assumptions and biases.

Furthermore, educators use reasoning techniques to cultivate creativity and innovation in the learning process. They aim to inspire students to think creatively and beyond conventional limits, explore multiple perspectives, and generate novel ideas. Educators can create a dynamic and enriching learning environment by applying logical reasoning to foster creativity.

This chapter will provide practical examples and exercises demonstrating specialized reasoning techniques' application in education. By engaging with these examples, readers will gain insights into how logical reasoning can be applied to curriculum design, critical thinking instruction, and fostering creativity in educational settings.

Other Professional Domains

While business and education represent significant domains where reasoning skills are crucial, it is essential to acknowledge that specialized reasoning techniques are applicable in various professional fields. Depending on the nature of the environment, different reasoning strategies and frameworks may be employed to address specific challenges.

For example, in the legal and ethical domains, rigorous logical reasoning is essential to analyze complex issues, assess arguments, and make moral judgments. Legal reason involves applying logic and legal principles to interpret statutes, research case law, and construct persuasive arguments. Ethical reasoning requires the application of moral tenets and logical analysis to address ethical dilemmas and make ethically sound decisions.

The scientific method is a systematic framework for logical reasoning in scientific research and experimentation. Scientists employ logical reasoning to formulate hypotheses, design experiments, collect and analyze data, and conclude. The scientific method enables researchers to uncover the underlying principles governing natural phenomena and advance knowledge in their respective fields. (Gauch, 2003)

In engineering, reasoning techniques such as root

cause analysis play a critical role in problem-solving. Engineers apply logical reasoning to identify the underlying causes of failures or malfunctions, enabling them to develop effective solutions and prevent future problems. Engineers can address complex challenges in various engineering disciplines by employing a systematic approach to problem-solving.

Critical Thinking in Digital Environments

In today's digital age, critical thinking extends beyond traditional domains. This section explores the challenges and opportunities of critical thinking in digital environments, such as social media, online platforms, and information overload. We discuss strategies for evaluating digital information, identifying misinformation and fake news, and maintaining a critical mindset in the digital realm. Through interactive activities and case studies, readers will gain the necessary skills to navigate digital spaces critically and make informed decisions amidst much online information.

THE IMPACT OF DIGITAL ENVIRONMENTS ON CRITICAL THINKING

- **Information Overload and Cognitive Load**
  With the abundance of online information, individuals often face the challenge of information overload. We will discuss how

information overload can overwhelm critical thinking abilities and hinder decision-making processes. Additionally, we will explore the concept of cognitive load and its impact on reasoning and problem-solving in digital environments.

- **The Rise of Misinformation and Fake News**

The proliferation of misinformation and fake news poses a significant threat to critical thinking in digital environments. We will examine the reasons behind the spread of misinformation, the techniques used to manipulate public opinion, and the consequences of consuming false information. By understanding the dynamics of misinformation, readers will be better equipped to discern reliable sources and separate fact from fiction.

STRATEGIES FOR EVALUATING DIGITAL INFORMATION

- **Source Evaluation and Authority**

One key aspect of critical thinking in digital environments is the ability to evaluate the credibility and authority of information sources. We will discuss criteria for assessing source reliability, including expertise, reputation, and transparency. By employing these strategies, readers can ensure that they rely on trustworthy sources for their decision-making processes.

- **Fact-Checking and Verifying Information**
  Verifying the accuracy of information is crucial in the digital realm. We will explore fact-checking techniques, including cross-referencing information from multiple sources, using fact-checking websites, and investigating the credentials of authors or organizations. By developing fact-checking skills, readers can effectively identify and counter false or misleading information.

- **Identifying Biases and Manipulation**
  Digital environments are rife with biases and manipulation attempts. We will delve into various types of preferences, such as confirmation and cognitive biases, and their impact on critical thinking. Additionally, we will discuss techniques used for manipulating information and how to recognize and counteract them. By being aware of biases and manipulation tactics, readers can approach digital communication with a discerning and sceptical mindset.

NAVIGATING SOCIAL MEDIA AND ONLINE PLATFORMS

- **Critical Evaluation of Social Media Content**

  Social media platforms have evolved into essential knowledge providers and present unique challenges. We will explore strategies for critically evaluating social media content, including analyzing the credibility of posters, examining engagement metrics, and considering the potential biases or agendas behind shared information. By applying critical thinking skills to social media content, readers can avoid being influenced by misinformation and make informed decisions.

- **Engaging in Constructive Online Discourse**

  Online platforms offer opportunities for engaging in discussions and sharing perspectives. We will discuss strategies for participating in constructive online discourse, including active listening, empathy, and respectful communication. By fostering a positive and open-minded approach to online discussions, readers can contribute to a more informed and inclusive digital environment.

Enhancing Reasoning Skills through Cognitive Tools and Technology

THE ROLE OF COGNITIVE TOOLS IN ENHANCING REASONING

- **Introduction to Cognitive Tools**

We will provide an overview of cognitive tools and their significance in enhancing reasoning skills. Cognitive tools encompass various software applications, digital platforms, and technological resources to support and augment cognitive processes. Individuals can improve their thinking, problem-solving, and decision-making abilities by utilizing cognitive tools.

- **Mind-Mapping Software for Organized Thinking**

Mind-mapping software visually represents ideas and concepts, facilitating organized thinking and information processing. We will discuss the benefits of using mind-mapping tools, explore different software options available, and provide practical tips on effectively utilizing mind maps to enhance reasoning and critical thinking.

- **Analytical Tools for Data Evaluation**

With the increasing availability of data, analytical tools play a crucial role in reasoning and decision-making processes. We will explore data analytics software and platforms, highlighting how they can aid in analyzing and interpreting complex data sets. By leveraging analytical tools, readers can make data-driven decisions and draw accurate conclusions.

ONLINE COLLABORATION PLATFORMS FOR COLLECTIVE REASONING

- **Collaborative Problem-Solving through Digital Platforms**

  Online collaboration platforms provide opportunities for collective reasoning and problem-solving. We will discuss the benefits of such media, enabling individuals to collaborate, exchange ideas, and jointly solve complex problems. Additionally, we will explore strategies for effective online collaboration, including fostering communication, managing tasks, and leveraging collective intelligence.

- **Virtual Meeting Tools for Engaging Discourse**

  Virtual meeting tools have revolutionized the way people communicate and collaborate remotely. We will discuss how these tools can facilitate engaging discourse, foster critical thinking, and encourage diverse perspectives. By harnessing the features of virtual meeting tools, readers can participate in meaningful discussions and leverage the power of collective reasoning.

BEST PRACTICES FOR UTILIZING COGNITIVE TOOLS AND TECHNOLOGY

- **Selecting Appropriate Tools for Specific Tasks**

  Choosing the right cognitive tools and technology for specific tasks is crucial for maximizing their impact. We will discuss factors to consider when selecting tools, including task requirements, user compatibility, and scalability. Readers can effectively integrate cognitive tools into their reasoning and problem-solving processes by understanding the importance of tool selection.

- **Balancing Human Reasoning with Technological Support**

  While cognitive tools and technology can enhance reasoning skills, it is essential to maintain a balance between human reasoning and technological support. We will explore how individuals can leverage technology as a supplement rather than a replacement for their critical thinking abilities. Readers can make the most of both by recognizing the complementary nature of human reasoning and technological tools.

- **Case Studies and Practical Examples**

  To illustrate the practical application of cognitive tools and technology in enhancing reasoning skills, this section will include case studies and practical examples. Readers will explore real-life scenarios where cognitive tools have been effectively utilized to support critical thinking, problem-solving, and decision-making processes. These case studies will provide insights into the diverse ways in which technology can augment reasoning abilities.

TAKEAWAY

The foundation of critical thinking is reasoning, and by understanding its principles, applying it to everyday situations, and utilizing specialized techniques, we enhance our necessary thinking skills and become adept problem solvers in various domains.

This chapter explored the power of reasoning and its role in developing critical thinking skills. We began by understanding the principles of logical reasoning, enabling us to evaluate arguments and draw logical conclusions. We learned how to apply analytical reasoning techniques to everyday situations through practical application, enhancing our ability to critically analyze information and make well-informed decisions. Furthermore, we recognized the importance of specialized reasoning techniques for specific domains, equipping ourselves with the tools to excel in diverse fields. By harnessing the power of reasoning, we unlock our full potential in critical thinking, paving the way for effective problem-solving and decision-making.

Now that we have explored the power of reasoning and its practical application, we are ready to dive into the realm of problem-solving strategies. In Chapter 4, we will introduce effective frameworks for problem-solving and engage in interactive exercises to develop our problem-solving skills. We will also address the transferability of these skills to different contexts, equipping ourselves with strategies to adapt and thrive in real-world challenges. Come with us on a venture to achieve proficiency in problem-solving and enhance our ability to think critically.

CHAPTER FOUR
PROBLEM-SOLVING STRATEGIES

Introducing Effective Problem-Solving Frameworks

Practical problem-solving is a critical skill that allows individuals to overcome challenges, make informed decisions, and drive innovation. To navigate the complex landscape of problem-solving, it is essential to have effective frameworks and methodologies that provide a structured approach to analyzing problems, generating solutions, and evaluating their effectiveness. This chapter will examine several well-known problem-solving techniques and frameworks that have proven effective across different domains and industries.

In the quest for practical problem-solving, having a structured approach is crucial. Introducing readers to various problem-solving frameworks gives them a solid foundation for tackling challenges systematically. These frameworks offer step-by-step methodologies and strategies that guide individuals through problem-solving.

One of the most widely recognized problem-solving frameworks is the scientific method. This method involves a systematic and empirical approach to gathering data, formulating hypotheses, conducting experiments, analyzing results, and concluding. By following the scientific method, individuals can approach problems with an objective and evidence-based mindset, ensuring that their solutions are grounded in reliable information.

Another valuable problem-solving framework is root cause analysis. This approach focuses on identifying the underlying causes of a problem rather than simply addressing its symptoms. By investigating the root causes, individuals can develop targeted and long-lasting solutions. Root cause analysis involves asking probing questions, conducting thorough investigations, and analyzing the relationships between various factors contributing to the problem.

Design thinking is a human-centred problem-solving framework emphasizing empathy, creativity, and collaboration. It entails comprehending the needs and perspectives of those affected by the problem, generating innovative ideas, prototyping and testing potential solutions, and iterating based on feedback. Design thinking encourages a non-linear approach to problem-solving, enabling individuals to explore multiple possibilities and embrace the iterative nature of the creative process.

Decision-making frameworks such as cost-benefit analysis and SWOT analysis provide individuals with structured approaches for evaluating options and making informed choices. Cost-benefit research involves weighing different solutions' potential benefits and drawbacks to determine the most favourable outcome. On the other hand, SWOT analysis assesses the strengths, weaknesses, opportunities, and threats associated with various options, helping individuals identify the best course of action.

By introducing readers to these effective problem-solving frameworks, we empower them to approach challenges with clarity and purpose. Understanding and applying these methodologies provide individuals with a roadmap for problem-solving, enabling them to break down complex issues into manageable steps and make well-informed decisions.

This chapter will delve deeper into each framework, providing clear explanations, practical examples, and case studies that illustrate their application in real-world scenarios. By engaging with these frameworks and understanding their strengths and limitations, readers will develop the skills and confidence to tackle problems head-on and find practical solutions.

Engaging Readers through Interactive Problem-Solving Exercises

Engaging readers through interactive problem-solving exercises is vital to this chapter, providing a hands-on and immersive learning experience. The activities simulate real-life scenarios that readers may encounter, allowing them to apply the problem-solving frameworks introduced earlier practically and meaningfully. By actively participating in these exercises, readers can better understand the problem-solving process and enhance their critical thinking skills.

The interactive problem-solving exercises will be structured in a step-by-step format, guiding readers through each stage of the problem-solving process. They will be presented with a scenario or a specific problem to solve, and they will be encouraged to analyze the situation, identify the key issues, and generate possible solutions. Through guided prompts and questions, readers will be challenged to think critically, consider alternative perspectives, and weigh the advantages and disadvantages of various ways.

These exercises foster active learning and reader engagement by providing opportunities for readers to think independently, make decisions, and reflect on their problem-solving strategies. By actively participating in the exercises, readers can gain practical experience in applying the problem-solving frameworks discussed earlier, enabling them to develop their problem-solving skills in a supportive and interactive environment.

Feedback and guidance will be provided throughout the process to enhance the effectiveness of the interactive exercises further. This feedback will help readers understand the strengths and weaknesses of their solutions, identify areas for improvement, and refine their problem-solving techniques. Additionally, the exercises may incorporate collaborative elements, allowing readers to engage in group discussions, brainstorming sessions, or peer evaluations, fostering teamwork and collective problem-solving.

The interactive problem-solving exercises will cover a range of scenarios and challenges spanning various domains and contexts. This diversity ensures readers can practice problem-solving skills in different situations, broadening their understanding and adaptability. Whether analyzing a business case study, addressing an educational dilemma, or navigating a complex technological problem, the exercises offer readers a comprehensive learning experience relevant to their lives and interests.

Readers can develop their problem-solving skills

dynamically and engagingly through these interactive exercises. They will gain confidence in approaching and solving complex problems and become better equipped to apply critical thinking and reasoning in their personal and professional lives. By actively participating in these exercises, readers can internalize the problem-solving strategies presented in this chapter, making the learning process more enjoyable and impactful.

Adapting Problem-Solving Skills to Different Contexts

Adapting problem-solving skills to different contexts is essential for effectively addressing the diverse challenges in various fields and industries. This section will explore strategies and techniques that enable readers to modify and apply their problem-solving skills in specific domains such as business, education, technology, healthcare, and more. By understanding each context's unique characteristics and requirements, readers will be better equipped to tackle complex problems and make informed decisions.

One of the critical aspects of adapting problem-solving skills to different contexts is recognizing the specific challenges and nuances associated with each domain. For example, in business, problem-solving often involves profitability, market trends, and competition considerations. On the other hand, in education, problem-solving may revolve around curriculum design, student engagement, and learning outcomes. By understanding the distinct aspects of each domain, readers can tailor their problem-solving approaches accordingly. (Van Aken & Berends, 2018)

Practical examples and case studies will be incorporated to facilitate the understanding and application of problem-solving skills in different contexts. These real-world scenarios will demonstrate how problem-solving frameworks and techniques can be adapted and utilized effectively. Readers will be able to observe the application of problem-solving strategies in various situations, gaining insights into the decision-making processes and problem-solving methods employed by experts in their respective fields.

Furthermore, this section will explore the specific strategies and techniques relevant to each domain. For instance, in technology, problem-solving often involves analyzing complex systems, identifying software bugs, or devising innovative solutions. Readers will learn about specialized problem-solving methodologies and tools that can be utilized in the technology industry. Similarly, in healthcare, problem-solving may involve diagnostic challenges, treatment planning, and patient care. The section will provide insights into the problem-solving techniques employed by healthcare professionals, highlighting the critical thinking skills required in this field.

By exploring the adaptation of problem-solving skills to different contexts, readers will develop a broader perspective on the versatility of these skills. They will realize that problem-solving is not limited to specific domains but can be applied across various industries and areas of expertise. This understanding will empower readers to confidently approach new challenges, knowing they possess the adaptable problem-solving skills necessary to navigate unfamiliar territory.

Practicing problem-solving skills in different contexts also fosters creativity and innovation. As readers adapt their problem-solving techniques to unique situations, they will be encouraged to think outside the box, consider alternative perspectives, and generate innovative solutions. This emphasis on creative problem-solving enhances readers' ability to tackle complex problems and fosters a mindset of continuous learning and improvement.

Ultimately, this section aims to equip readers with the knowledge and strategies to effectively adapt their problem-solving skills to different contexts. By understanding the specific challenges, employing domain-specific methodologies, and drawing inspiration from practical examples, readers will develop the flexibility and adaptability needed to thrive in a rapidly changing world.

Developing Creative Problem-Solving Skills

Developing creative problem-solving skills is crucial for individuals seeking to master the art of critical thinking and effective decision-making. Creativity enables us to break free from traditional thinking patterns, explore alternative possibilities, and generate innovative solutions to complex problems. This section will explore various techniques and strategies to foster and enhance creative problem-solving skills.

One of the fundamental techniques for cultivating creativity in problem-solving is brainstorming. Brainstorming encourages generating a wide range of ideas by suspending judgment and promoting a free flow of thoughts. Individuals can unleash their creativity and develop novel problem-solving approaches by creating a supportive and non-judgmental environment. We will explore different brainstorming techniques, such as group brainstorming, individual brainstorming, and structured brainstorming methods like the SCAMPER technique or the six thinking hats approach.

Another effective tool for stimulating creative problem-solving is mind mapping. Mind mapping allows individuals to visually organize their thoughts, ideas, and connections to a specific problem or topic. People can uncover new insights and generate innovative solutions by mapping associations and relationships. We will explore the principles of mind mapping and provide practical guidance on creating and utilizing mind maps effectively in problem-solving scenarios.

Lateral thinking is another valuable approach to fostering creativity in problem-solving. Coined by Edward de Bono, lateral thinking involves thinking beyond conventional boundaries and exploring unconventional angles and perspectives. It encourages individuals to challenge assumptions, seek alternative viewpoints, and find innovative solutions. We will delve into various techniques associated with lateral thinking, such as random word stimulation, provocation techniques, and applying the "six thinking hats" method.

In addition to specific techniques, cultivating a growth mindset is essential for developing creative problem-solving skills. A growth mindset holds that intelligence and abilities may be set through effort, effort, and continuous learning. By adopting a growth mindset, individuals are more open to embracing challenges, persisting in the face of obstacles, and seeking new strategies when faced with setbacks. We will explore strategies for fostering a growth mindset, such as embracing failure as a learning opportunity, seeking feedback and constructive criticism, and cultivating a passion for lifelong learning.

Throughout this section, we will provide practical examples and case studies that demonstrate the application of creative problem-solving techniques in real-life situations. These examples will highlight the transformative power of creativity in generating breakthrough solutions and tackling complex challenges. By understanding and applying these techniques, readers can tap into their creative potential, approach problems with fresh perspectives, and unlock innovative solutions.

Moreover, developing creative problem-solving skills enhances individual problem-solving abilities and promotes innovation and collaboration within teams and organizations. Creative problem-solving fosters an environment where diverse ideas are valued, encourages collaboration and collective intelligence, and drives continuous improvement and innovation.

In conclusion, developing creative problem-solving skills is crucial for individuals interested in mastering the art of critical thinking and effective problem-solving. By exploring techniques such as brainstorming, mind mapping, lateral thinking, and fostering a growth mindset, readers can unlock their creative potential and approach challenges with fresh perspectives. The practical application of these techniques, real-life examples, and case studies will inspire readers to embrace creativity as a powerful tool for generating innovative solutions.

Enhancing Collaborative Problem-Solving

Enhancing collaborative problem-solving skills is essential for individuals seeking to navigate complex challenges and capitalize on a group's collective intelligence. This section will explore strategies and techniques for effective collaboration and teamwork in problem-solving scenarios.

Effective communication is a cornerstone of collaborative problem-solving. We will delve into communication strategies that foster understanding, active listening, and constructive dialogue within teams. Techniques such as active listening, paraphrasing, and asking clarifying questions will be explored to ensure clear and effective communication among team members. Additionally, we will discuss the importance of empathy and respect in fostering a positive team dynamic where all members feel valued and heard.

Team dynamics play a crucial role in collaborative problem-solving. We will examine the roles individuals can assume within a team, such as the facilitator, the idea generator, the critical thinker, and the implementer. Understanding these roles and their respective contributions will enable readers to effectively leverage team members' diverse strengths and skills. Moreover, we will explore techniques for managing conflicts and fostering a collaborative and inclusive team culture.

Tools and technologies can significantly enhance collaboration in problem-solving. We will explore digital devices and platforms facilitating communication, information sharing, and collaboration. These tools may include project management software, virtual collaboration platforms, and online brainstorming tools. By leveraging these tools effectively, individuals can overcome geographical barriers and collaborate seamlessly, even in remote or virtual settings.

Case studies and interactive activities will be incorporated to provide practical examples of collaborative problem-solving in action. Readers can engage in simulated problem-solving scenarios, working in teams to address complex challenges. These activities will enhance their problem-solving skills and provide valuable insights into the dynamics of effective collaboration. By experiencing firsthand the power of collective intelligence and teamwork, readers will gain the confidence and ability to apply collaborative problem-solving techniques in real-world situations.

Furthermore, fostering a culture of collaboration within organizations and teams is crucial for sustained success in problem-solving endeavours. We will explore strategies for creating a teamwork environment, such as encouraging open communication, recognizing and valuing diverse perspectives, and establishing a shared sense of purpose and trust among team members. By cultivating a collaborative culture, organizations can tap into the full potential of their teams and foster an environment where innovative solutions emerge naturally.

TAKEAWAY

Effective problem-solving requires a structured approach and the utilization of appropriate frameworks and techniques. This chapter has explored several effective problem-solving frameworks that can guide individuals in analyzing problems, generating solutions, and making informed decisions. Readers can enhance their problem-solving skills and approach challenges with a systematic and organized mindset by understanding and applying the scientific method, root cause analysis, design thinking, and decision-making frameworks.

Moreover, we have witnessed the power of inquiry through the scientific method, the importance of identifying root causes through root cause analysis, the value of empathy and creativity in design thinking, and the significance of informed decision-making through cost-benefit analysis and SWOT analysis. These frameworks and approaches can be applied in various domains and contexts, enabling individuals to address complex problems effectively and drive meaningful solutions.

Moving forward to Chapter 5, "Analyzing Information and Making Informed Decisions," we will build upon the problem-solving foundations established thus far and explore the skills and techniques necessary to critically evaluate information, avoid cognitive biases, and make sound decisions based on reliable evidence. Let us embark on this next chapter, where we will equip readers with the tools to navigate information overload and make informed choices in an increasingly complex world.

CHAPTER FIVE
EVALUATING THE CREDIBILITY
OF INFORMATION SOURCES

Evaluating the credibility of information sources is a crucial skill in the age of abundant information and digital media. With the proliferation of online platforms and the ease of sharing information, it has become increasingly challenging to distinguish reliable sources from misinformation and biased content. In this section, we will delve into the principles and techniques for evaluating the credibility of information sources. By understanding the key factors determining credibility and employing critical evaluation strategies, readers can make informed decisions and navigate the vast sea of information more effectively.

❖ **The Importance of Source Credibility:** To start, it is essential to establish why evaluating the credibility of information sources is vital. Information is readily available in today's interconnected world, but not all citations are trustworthy. We will explore the potential consequences of relying on unreliable or biased information and highlight the importance of discerning credible sources to ensure accuracy, objectivity, and validity.

❖ **Assessing Source Reliability:** When evaluating the credibility of an information source, one of the critical considerations is its reliability. In this section, we will discuss various factors that contribute to source reliability. These may include the authors or organization's reputation and expertise, the publication or platform where the information is shared, and peer review or editorial oversight. We will explore strategies for assessing the reliability of sources and provide practical guidelines for readers to apply in their research.

❖ **Recognizing Bias and Conflicts of Interest:** Bias can significantly impact the credibility of information sources. We will explore different types of bias, such as political, commercial, and ideological, and discuss how they can influence the presentation and interpretation of information. By understanding the signs of bias and conflicts of interest, readers can identify potential pitfalls and critically evaluate the information they encounter.

❖ **Fact-Checking and Verification:** In an era of rapid information sharing, fact-checking has become essential for evaluating credibility. We will introduce readers to fact-checking techniques and resources, including reputable fact-checking organizations and online tools. We will review the significance of confirming information from numerous sources and provide practical tips for effective fact-checking.

❖ **Navigating Digital and Social Media Sources:** With the prevalence of digital platforms and social media, evaluating the credibility of online sources has become increasingly complex. We will address the challenges of user-generated content, misinformation spread, and algorithms' influence. Readers will gain insights into strategies for critically assessing information shared through digital channels and cautiously navigating the digital landscape.

❖ **Case Studies and Examples:** To demonstrate the principles presented in this section, we will give real-world case studies and examples. These case studies will cover various topics, including news articles, scientific research, social media posts, and online forums. By analyzing these examples, readers will develop critical evaluation skills and learn to apply the principles and techniques discussed in real-life scenarios.

Identifying reliable and trustworthy sources of information

Identifying reliable and trustworthy sources of information is a crucial skill in the age of abundant information and digital media. With the vast amount of information available at our fingertips, it becomes increasingly important to discern between reliable sources and those that may be inaccurate, biased, or misleading. In this section, we will explore strategies and criteria for evaluating the credibility and trustworthiness of information sources. By understanding these techniques, readers can make informed decisions and avoid misinformation.

❖ **The Importance of Source Evaluation:** In today's digital landscape, where information is easily accessible and can be shared by anyone, the importance of source evaluation cannot be overstated. Recognizing the potential consequences of relying on unreliable or biased sources is essential. Making decisions based on false information can have significant implications in various aspects of life, including personal choices, professional endeavours, and societal impact. By highlighting the significance of source evaluation, readers will understand the need for critical thinking and discernment when assessing the reliability of information sources.

❖ **Evaluating Source Authority and Expertise:** An essential aspect of assessing the credibility of information sources is evaluating the authority and expertise of the author or organization providing the information. Readers will be introduced to strategies for determining the source's qualifications, credentials, and expertise. This includes considering the author's educational background, professional experience, affiliations, and track record of publishing reliable information. By scrutinizing the author's qualifications and expertise, readers can gauge the reliability of the data presented.

❖ **Assessing Source Objectivity and Bias:** Objectivity is an essential criterion when evaluating the trustworthiness of a source. Readers will discover techniques for identifying bias in information sources in this section. We will delve into different types of discrimination, such as political, ideological, commercial, or personal bias, and how they can influence the presentation of information. By examining the language used, the inclusion or exclusion of certain information, and the presence of any potential conflicts of interest, readers will learn to analyze the objectivity of sources critically.

❖ **Fact-Checking and Verification:** In today's age of "fake news" and misinformation, fact-checking plays a crucial role in evaluating source reliability. Readers will explore various techniques and resources for fact-checking information in this section. We will emphasize the importance of cross-referencing information with multiple sources to verify its accuracy. By seeking corroboration from reputable and authoritative sources, readers can gain confidence in the reliability of the information they encounter.

❖ **Utilizing Online Tools and Resources:** The digital age has brought forth various online tools and resources that can assist in evaluating source reliability. This section introduces readers to online platforms and fact-checking websites that provide trustworthy information and help identify misinformation. We will explore the features and functionalities of these tools, emphasizing their role in promoting transparency and accountability.

Assessing the credibility and expertise of authors or organizations

In the digital age, where information is readily available, assessing the credibility and expertise of authors or organizations is crucial. With so much information on the internet, developing the skills to discern reliable and trustworthy sources from those that may be biased, inaccurate, or lacking authority is essential. This section will delve into strategies and considerations for assessing the credibility and expertise of authors or organizations, equipping readers with the tools they need to make informed decisions about the information they encounter.

Several factors come into play when evaluating the credibility of authors or organizations. First and foremost is the author's expertise and qualifications in the subject matter. It is essential to consider the author's educational background, professional experience, and any relevant credentials they possess. These factors can provide valuable insights into their level of knowledge and expertise.

Furthermore, assessing the author's reputation and recognition within the field is essential. This can be done by researching their previous publications, affiliations with reputable institutions or organizations, and any awards or accolades they may have received. Recognized experts and thought leaders in a particular domain are more likely to produce reliable and authoritative content.

Another aspect to consider is the author's or organization's objectivity and potential biases. Everyone has their perspectives and preferences; It is also critical to be mindful of potential conflicts of interest that may influence the information supplied.

Transparent disclosure of affiliations, funding sources, or potential conflicts positively indicates credibility.

The publication or platform hosting the information also plays a role in evaluating credibility. Reputable publishers, academic journals, and established news outlets typically have rigorous editorial processes and fact-checking mechanisms. They adhere to specific standards of quality and accuracy, making their content more reliable than self-published or unverified sources.

In addition to evaluating the author or organization, it is crucial to examine the content critically. Look for evidence-based claims supported by reputable sources, citations, or references. Verify whether the information is up-to-date, as outdated information can be misleading or irrelevant. Consistency and coherence in the argumentation also indicate a well-supported and credible work. It is worth mentioning that the digital landscape has its challenges when it comes to assessing credibility. Plenty of misinformation, clickbait headlines, and fabricated content necessitates a vigilant approach. Assessing the credibility and expertise of authors or organizations websites, online databases, and reviews from reputable experts or organizations can provide valuable insights into the credibility and accuracy of a source.

Developing the skills to assess credibility and expertise takes time and practice. It requires a critical mindset, a willingness to question and verify information, and a commitment to seeking reliable sources. By honing these skills, readers can confidently navigate the vast sea of information, ensuring that the knowledge they acquire is trustworthy and informed.

In conclusion, evaluating the credibility and expertise of authors or organizations is a vital skill in the information age. By considering factors such as expertise, reputation, objectivity, and the quality of the publication, readers can make informed decisions about the credibility of the material they come across. Engaging in critical thinking and actively seeking reliable sources empowers individuals to make well-informed decisions. It ensures they can rely on accurate and trustworthy information for their personal and professional endeavors.

Recognizing bias and potential conflicts of interest
Recognizing bias and potential conflicts of interest is crucial in analyzing information and making informed decisions. It involves the ability to identify subjective influences and external factors that may impact the objectivity and reliability of the data presented.

When evaluating information sources, readers should be mindful of the potential bias that authors or organizations may have. Discrimination can arise from personal beliefs, values, or affiliations and influence how information is presented or interpreted. As readers, it is essential to critically assess the author's background and any potential conflicts of interest.

For example, let's consider a scenario where Astraean Bach, a renowned climate change researcher, publishes an article on the effects of global warming. Recognizing bias and potential conflicts of interest in this context would involve considering Astraean Bach's professional background and affiliations. Suppose Astraean Bach has received funding from organizations or industries with a vested interest in downplaying the impact of global warming. In that case, readers should be aware of the potential bias and carefully evaluate the information provided.

Moreover, recognizing bias goes beyond just identifying explicit conflicts of interest. It also involves awareness of implicit cultural, societal, or personal preferences. These biases can influence how information is framed, the selection of data, or the omission of specific perspectives. By being mindful of these biases, readers can approach information critically and seek a more comprehensive and balanced understanding.

Recognizing bias and potential conflicts of

interest requires readers to be vigilant in assessing the background and affiliations of authors and organizations. By doing so, readers can better evaluate the objectivity and reliability of the information presented and make more informed decisions based on a well-rounded understanding of the topic at hand.

Analyzing Data and Statistics

This section will equip readers with the necessary skills to analyze and evaluate data effectively, enabling them to draw accurate conclusions and avoid common pitfalls.

The process of analyzing data begins with understanding the basics of data interpretation. Readers will learn about different data types, such as quantitative and qualitative data, and the appropriate methods for analyzing each type. They will gain familiarity with statistical concepts, mean, median, mode, standard deviation, and correlation, for example, are essential for extracting meaningful insights from data.

Moreover, readers will develop the ability to recognize common statistical fallacies and misinterpretations. They will learn to identify potential biases or errors in data collection and analysis, allowing them to approach data with a critical eye. By understanding these pitfalls, readers can avoid drawing incorrect or misleading conclusions from data, ensuring their selections are based on precise and dependable information.

Visualizing data is another crucial aspect of data analysis. Readers will explore various data visualization techniques, such as charts, graphs, and infographics, that facilitate information's clear and concise presentation. They will learn to select the most appropriate visualization method for different data types and effectively communicate their findings through visual representations.

Real-world examples and case studies will demonstrate the practical application of data analysis in different contexts. Readers will be encouraged to actively engage with data sets and practice their analytical skills through interactive activities. These activities will involve interpreting and drawing conclusions from data, identifying trends and patterns, and evaluating the reliability and validity of data sources.

Understanding the basics of data interpretation

Understanding the basics of data interpretation is essential for effectively analyzing information and making informed decisions. In this section, readers will learn the fundamental principles and concepts that form the foundation of data interpretation.

First and foremost, readers explore the different types of data commonly encountered in various contexts. They will become familiar with quantitative data, which consists of numerical measurements and can be analyzed using statistical techniques. Additionally, readers will learn about qualitative data, which involves non-numerical information such as observations, interviews, or textual data, and requires different analysis methods.

Next, readers will delve into the data collection process and its impact on interpretation. They will understand the importance of reliable and unbiased data sources and the potential limitations and biases that can arise during data collection. By recognizing these factors, readers can critically evaluate the quality and credibility of the data they encounter.

This part will also address statistical ideas and metrics. Readers will learn about central tendency metrics such as the mean, median, and mode., which provide insight into a dataset's typical values. They will also investigate dispersion measurements such as range and standard deviation, which describe the variability or spread of the data. Readers can grasp the properties of a dataset and make meaningful comparisons if they understand these statistical measurements.

Readers will be introduced to graphical data representations in addition to numerical metrics. They will learn to design and understand charts, graphs, and diagrams that effectively explain data patterns, trends, and relationships. Data visualization in graphical form can help with comprehension and identification.

Data visualization in graphical form can improve comprehension and facilitate the identification of critical insights. This part will include practical examples and exercises to help you remember the principles and practices you've learned. Readers can interact with datasets, use statistical measures, and evaluate the results. They will improve their understanding and analysis skills by actively engaging with data.

Ultimately, understanding the basics of data interpretation equips readers to extract meaning from data, identify patterns and trends, and draw valid conclusions. This skill is crucial for making informed decisions based on reliable evidence and avoiding the pitfalls of misinterpretation. By honing their data interpretation skills, readers will become more effective critical thinkers and problem solvers in a data-driven environment.

Recognizing Common Statistical Fallacies and Misinterpretations

Understanding statistics is crucial for analyzing information and making informed decisions. However, statistical data can be misleading if not correctly interpreted. This section will focus on common statistical fallacies and misinterpretations that individuals should be aware of. By recognizing and understanding these fallacies, readers will be better equipped to evaluate statistical information critically. Here are some key points to explore:

❖ **Correlation vs Causation:** Understanding the distinction between correlation (two variables changing together) and causation (one variable causing a change in another) and explaining how mistaking correlation for causation can lead to incorrect conclusions.

❖ **Sample Size and Representativeness:** Highlighting the importance of sample size in statistical analysis and discussing how small or biased samples can lead to misleading results. I am exploring the concept of representative sampling and its role in drawing accurate conclusions.

❖ **Misleading Graphs and Charts:** Discuss common graphical misrepresentations, such as improper scaling, truncated axes, and manipulated visualizations that distort data. It provides examples and guidelines for interpreting graphs and charts accurately.

❖ **Simpson's Paradox:** Explaining the phenomenon of Simpson's paradox, where trends observed in subgroups of data are reversed or distorted when the data is analyzed as a whole. They illustrate how this can lead to misleading interpretations if not adequately understood.

❖ **Statistical Significance and P-values:** Clarifying the meaning and interpretation of statistical significance and p-values in hypothesis testing and discussing the limitations and potential misinterpretations associated with relying solely on p-values.

❖ **Confirmation Bias in Statistical Interpretation:** Highlighting how confirmation bias can influence the interpretation of statistical data, leading to selective attention and cherry-picking of evidence and discussing strategies to mitigate confirmation bias in statistical analysis.

❖ **Misrepresentation of Risk and Probability:** Exploring common errors in communicating and understanding risk and probability, such as neglecting base rates, framing effects, and the use of absolute vs relative risk and guiding how to interpret and communicate risk-related information accurately. By addressing these common statistical fallacies and misinterpretations, readers will develop a critical eye when encountering statistical information. They can identify potential pitfalls and make more educated decisions based on a solid statistical grasp. Practical examples, case studies, and interactive exercises can be incorporated to reinforce the concepts and engage readers in active learning.

Using data visualization techniques to enhance understanding

Data visualization is valuable for information analysis and presenting complex data clearly and intuitively. This section will explore data visualization techniques to enhance understanding and facilitate informed decision-making. By effectively visualizing data, readers can grasp patterns, relationships, and trends more quickly. Here are some key points to consider:

Importance of Visualizing Data: Discussing the benefits of data visualization in understanding complex information. Explaining how visual representations can simplify data, reveal patterns, and convey insights that might be difficult to grasp through raw data alone.

Choosing the Right Visualization: Exploring different data visualizations, such as bar charts, line graphs, scatter plots, heat maps, and infographics. Providing guidelines on selecting the most appropriate visualization based on the nature of the data and the intended message.

Design Principles for Effective Data Visualization: Discuss design principles for visually appealing and informative visualizations. We are exploring concepts such as clarity, simplicity, color selection, labelling, and appropriate use of visual elements (e.g., size, shape, position).

Interactive Data Visualization: Introducing interactive data visualization tools and techniques that allow users to explore and interact with data. They discussed the benefits of interactivity in uncovering insights and enabling users to customize their data exploration experience.

Storytelling with Data: Highlighting the power of storytelling in data visualization. Explaining how narrative elements, such as titles, captions, annotations, and contextual information, can guide readers through the data and convey a compelling story.

Visualizing Uncertainty: Discuss techniques for representing uncertainty in data visualizations, such as error bars, confidence intervals, and probabilistic visualizations. Visualizing uncertainty can provide a more comprehensive understanding of data and aid in decision-making under uncertainty.

Ethical Considerations in Data Visualization:
Addressing ethical considerations related to data visualization, such as avoiding misleading visual representations, presenting data in a fair and unbiased manner, and respecting privacy and confidentiality.

By incorporating effective data visualization techniques, readers can explore and understand complex information more effectively. Practical examples, hands-on exercises, and interactive visualization tools can engage readers and provide opportunities for applying data visualization principles in real-world scenarios.

Identifying and Addressing Cognitive Biases

This section will delve deeper into common cognitive biases significantly influencing our decision-making processes. By understanding these biases, readers will become more aware of the potential mistakes and difficulties they may face, allowing them to make more informed and rational decisions. Some of the critical cognitive biases we will explore include the following:

Confirmation Bias:
The tendency to search for, interpret, or favour information that confirms our preexisting beliefs or hypotheses.

How confirmation bias can hinder critical thinking and objective analysis by limiting exposure to alternative perspectives.

Strategies to overcome confirmation bias include actively seeking contradictory evidence and considering multiple viewpoints.

Availability Heuristic:
The tendency to rely on immediate examples or easily accessible information when making judgments or decisions.

How the availability heuristic can lead to biased assessments of probability or risk.

Techniques to mitigate the istic influx heuristics influence.

Anchoring Bias:
When forming judgments or estimates, there is a tendency to rely too strongly on the initial information received. How can anchoring bias lead to a skewed evaluation of subsequent information or options?

Strategies to mitigate the impact of anchoring bias, such as considering multiple reference points or recalibrating initial estimates.

Recognizing how biases influence perception and judgment.

Building on exploring cognitive biases, this section will focus on understanding how biases can shape our perception and judgment. By identifying the influence of biases, readers can develop a more objective and balanced approach to evaluating information and making decisions. We will explore the following:

Bias Awareness:
We are developing an awareness of our biases and their potential impact on decision-making.

We recognize the role of unconscious biases in shaping perceptions and judgments.

Techniques for self-reflection and introspection to identify and challenge biases.

Impact on Evaluation:
How biases can affect our evaluations of people, events, or information.

The role of preferences in forming stereotypes, making generalizations, or relying on snap judgments.

Strategies for mitigating evaluation biases include using objective criteria and seeking diverse perspectives.

Developing strategies to mitigate the effects of cognitive biases.

In this part, we will supply readers with information on practical strategies to reduce the impact of cognitive biases and make more objective and rational decisions. By implementing these strategies, readers can overcome the limitations of preferences and improve their critical thinking and decision-making skills. Some of the systems we will explore include:

Critical Thinking Skills:

Enhancing critical thinking skills to question assumptions, evaluate evidence, and consider alternative viewpoints.

Techniques for analyzing information objectively and making logical, evidence-based decisions.

The importance of cultivating an open and curious mindset to challenge biases.

Decision-Making Tools:

It introduces decision-making tools and frameworks that provide a structured approach to evaluating options and making decisions.

How decision-making tools can help mitigate the influence of biases by promoting systematic analysis and considering multiple factors.

Seeking Diverse Perspectives:

We encourage exploring diverse perspectives

and opinions to counteract biases and broaden understanding.

Strategies for actively seeking different viewpoints, engaging in constructive dialogue, and considering alternative solutions.

By adopting these strategies and approaches, readers can develop a more objective and rational decision-making process. They will be better equipped to navigate the complexities of bias and make more informed choices grounded in evidence and critical thinking.

Critical Thinking in Problem Identification

Effective problem-solving begins with the identification and definition of the problem at hand. In this section, we will explore the crucial role of critical thinking in this initial problem-solving stage. By applying necessary thinking skills, readers will gain the ability to analyze situations, evaluate information, and identify the significant issues that must be addressed.

To delve deeper into this topic, we will draw insights from the book "Think Smarter: Critical Thinking to Improve Problem-Solving and Decision-Making Skills" by M. Kallet (2014). This valuable resource provides practical guidance on how to enhance critical thinking skills and apply them in the context of problem identification.

Kallet, M. (2014). Think Smarter: Critical Thinking to Improve Problem-Solving and Decision-Making Skills. John Wiley & Sons.

❖ **The Importance of Critical Thinking in Problem Identification:**

Understanding how critical thinking enhances the problem-solving process.

The role of critical thinking in identifying problems accurately and comprehensively.

How critical thinking helps to avoid superficial or misguided problem identification.

❖ **Techniques for Framing and Clarifying Problem Statements:**

Exploring strategies and approaches to framing problem statements clearly and precisely.

The significance of defining problem boundaries and scope to ensure focused problem-solving efforts.

We are utilizing critical thinking to identify relevant factors and stakeholders involved in the problem.

❖ Uncovering Underlying Causes and Root Issues:

It recognizes the difference between symptoms and underlying causes of problems.

Applying critical thinking skills to dig deeper and uncover the root causes behind complex issues.

We are utilizing tools such as root cause analysis, cause-and-effect diagrams, and the 5 Whys technique to identify the fundamental reasons contributing to the problem.

❖ Analyzing Problem Context and Factors:

We are examining the importance of considering the broader context in problem identification.

We are applying critical thinking to assess the various factors contributing to the problem.

Identifying external influences, internal dynamics, and other relevant contextual elements shapes the problem.

❖ Questioning Assumptions and Biases:

It understands how assumptions and biases can hinder accurate problem identification.

We are utilizing critical thinking to question assumptions and challenge preconceived notions.

We are recognizing and mitigating the impact of personal and cognitive biases on problem identification.

❖ Gathering and Analyzing Relevant Information:

We discussed strategies for gathering and analyzing relevant information to support problem identification.

We are applying critical thinking to assess the reliability and credibility of information sources.

We use analytical tools and techniques to analyze data and extract meaningful insights.

❖ Collaborative Problem Identification:

Exploring the benefits of collaborative problem identification processes. Leveraging diverse perspectives and expertise through group discussions and brainstorming sessions.

We apply critical thinking to facilitate collaborative problem identification and reach a consensus.

❖ Ethical Considerations in Problem Identification:

Recognizing the ethical dimensions of problem identification. Applying critical thinking to ensure fairness and inclusivity and considering potential impacts on stakeholders.

Discussing ethical frameworks and guidelines for ethical problem identification practices.

❖ Ethical Considerations in Decision-Making:

We are highlighting the importance of ethical considerations in the decision-making process.

They are exploring the ethical dimensions of decision-making and their impact on individuals and society.

We discussed the significance of aligning decisions with moral values and principles.

❖ Ethical Frameworks and Principles for Decision-Making:

Introducing different ethical frameworks, such as consequentialism, deontology, and virtue ethics.

I am exploring the principles that guide ethical decision-making, such as fairness, justice, and integrity.

We discussed how ethical frameworks and principles can be applied to decision-making processes.

❖ Analyzing Ethical Dilemmas:

They present various ethical dilemmas that

individuals may encounter in decision-making situations.

I am exploring the complexities and conflicting interests involved in ethical dilemmas.

We discussed the importance of recognizing and addressing ethical dilemmas systematically and thoughtfully.

❖ **Strategies for Ethical Decision-Making:**
Providing strategies and approaches for making ethical decisions.

Discussing methods for evaluating the ethical implications of different options.

We are exploring the importance of considering long-term consequences and the well-being of stakeholders in ethical decision-making.

❖ **Balancing Ethical Considerations with Practical Constraints:**
Addressing the challenges of balancing ethical considerations with practical constraints, such as time, resources, and conflicting interests.

We discussed techniques for finding common ground between ethical principles and practical realities.

We are exploring strategies for effectively communicating and justifying ethical decisions to stakeholders.

By exploring these sections, readers will gain a deeper understanding of the ethical dimensions of decision-making processes. They will become familiar with ethical frameworks and principles that can guide their decision-making and develop the skills to analyze and address ethical dilemmas. Ultimately, readers will be equipped to make informed and ethically sound decisions that consider the interests of all stakeholders involved.

Conclusion:

In conclusion, Chapter 5 has focused on the critical skills of analyzing information and making informed decisions. We began by emphasizing the importance of critically evaluating information sources to ensure their credibility and reliability. Readers can navigate potential misinformation and make well-informed judgments by recognizing common pitfalls and cognitive biases.

Furthermore, interactive activities have been incorporated to provide readers with hands-on experience analyzing real-world scenarios and applying their critical thinking skills to make informed decisions. These activities have allowed readers to practice evaluating information, weighing different perspectives, and considering the implications of their choices.

Throughout this chapter, we have emphasized the significance of critical thinking in the decision-making process. By employing logical reasoning, avoiding biases, and examining ethical considerations, readers are better equipped to approach decision-making thoughtfully and responsibly.

TAKEAWAY

The key takeaway from this chapter is that effective decision-making relies on critical evaluation, avoiding biases, and considering ethical implications. By cultivating these skills, readers can navigate the abundance of information, separate fact from fiction, and make well-informed decisions that align with their values and goals.

In the upcoming chapter, we will explore the role of creativity and innovation in problem-solving. We will delve into techniques for cultivating creative thinking skills, overcoming creative blocks, and fostering an environment encouraging innovation. By embracing creativity and approaching problem-solving from a fresh perspective, readers will unlock new possibilities and discover unique solutions to their challenges.

We will introduce various creative problem-solving techniques and provide practical examples from different domains to illustrate their application. Additionally, interactive exercises and case studies will allow readers to engage with the material and enhance their problem-solving abilities actively.

Join us in Chapter 6 as we embark on a journey of creativity and innovation, expanding our problem-solving toolkit and unlocking the transformative power of thinking outside the box.

CHAPTER SIX
CREATIVITY AND INNOVATION IN PROBLEM-SOLVING

Cultivating Creative Thinking Skills

This section focuses on cultivating creative thinking skills as a foundation for problem-solving and innovation. By developing these skills, readers will unlock their creative potential and approach problem-solving with fresh perspectives and ideas.

Nurturing a Growth Mindset: Embracing a mindset that values curiosity, learning, and embracing challenges.

The power of mindset: Understanding the difference between fixed and growth mindset and its impact on creativity.

Embracing challenges: Encourage readers to see hurdles rather than as challenges to overcome. Cultivating curiosity: Fostering a sense of wonder and curiosity about the world, which fuels creative thinking and exploration.

Stimulating Imagination and Divergent Thinking: Techniques such as brainstorming, mind mapping, and free association generate various ideas.

Brainstorming: Exploring the concept of brainstorming and techniques for generating many ideas without judgment.

Mind mapping: Using visual diagrams to capture and connect ideas, stimulating connections and associations that spark creativity.

Free association: Encouraging readers to explore unconventional connections between ideas, allowing their thoughts to flow freely and form unexpected associations.

Embracing Unconventional Approaches: Encouraging readers to challenge conventional thinking patterns and explore alternative perspectives.

Breaking mental barriers: Overcoming self-imposed limitations and embracing the freedom to think beyond traditional boundaries.

Seeking diverse perspectives: Recognizing the value of diverse viewpoints and actively seeking different perspectives to expand thinking.

Embracing ambiguity and uncertainty: Being

comfortable with ambiguity and embracing uncertainty as a catalyst for creative problem-solving.

Fostering a Creative Environment: Creating an environment that supports and nurtures creativity.

Cultivating curiosity and exploration: Encouraging an environment that fosters curiosity and allows for exploring new ideas and possibilities.

Encouraging risk-taking: Creating a safe space where readers feel comfortable taking risks and embracing the potential for failure as a learning opportunity.

Providing resources and inspiration: Offering access to resources, such as books, articles, workshops, and inspiring examples, to stimulate creativity and provide inspiration.

Practicing Reflection and Iteration: Emphasizing the importance of reflection and iteration in the creative process.

Reflecting on experiences: Encouraging readers to reflect on their experiences and extract lessons learned to inform future creative endeavors.

Iterative problem-solving: Promoting an iterative approach to problem-solving, where ideas are continually refined and improved through feedback and reflection.

Embracing failure as a steppingstone: Helping readers understand that failure is an inherent part of the creative process and can lead to valuable insights and breakthroughs.

Nurturing Collaborative Creativity: Harnessing the power of collaboration to enhance creative thinking.

Building a creative team: Exploring strategies for building diverse teams that bring together individuals with different perspectives, skills, and backgrounds.

Facilitating effective collaboration: Providing tools and techniques, including brainstorming sessions, idea sharing, and constructive feedback.

Celebrating collective achievements: Recognizing and celebrating the team's accomplishments, fostering a culture of collaboration and support.

By cultivating a creative environment, practicing reflection and iteration, and nurturing collaborative creativity, readers will develop creative thinking skills and unlock innovation potential. They will be equipped to approach problem-solving with fresh perspectives, break through creative blocks, and apply innovative problem-solving techniques effectively.

Exploring Alternative Perspectives: Encouraging readers to challenge their assumptions and explore alternative perspectives to foster innovative thinking.

I am embracing Failure as a Learning Opportunity: Shifting the perception of failure as a setback to viewing it as a valuable learning experience that can lead to growth and innovation.

Promoting Continuous Learning: Cultivating a mindset of lifelong learning and continuous improvement to stay open to new ideas and adapt to changing circumstances.

We encourage Interdisciplinary Thinking: Breaking down silos and promoting integrating knowledge and ideas from different disciplines to foster innovation and creative problem-solving.

Nurturing a Culture of Innovation: Developing strategies for creating an organizational culture that values and promotes innovation, including incentives for creativity, open communication channels, and support for experimentation.

Applying Creative Problem-Solving Techniques to Specific Domains
Creative Problem-Solving in Business

Organizations must be creative and innovative to remain competitive in today's quickly changing business world. This subsection will explore how creative problem-solving techniques can be applied in business. We will delve into innovative approaches to product development, marketing strategies, and problem-solving in the business context. Readers will gain insights into methods such as design thinking, ideation processes, and innovation frameworks that can help organizations identify opportunities, generate creative ideas, and implement innovative solutions. Practical examples and case studies will illustrate how businesses have leveraged creative problem-solving to drive growth, improve customer experiences and acquire a competitive advantage.

Creativity in Education and Learning

Education is crucial in nurturing creative thinking and fostering a culture of innovation. This subsection will explore how creativity can be integrated into educational settings. We will examine how innovative problem-solving techniques can be applied to curriculum design, teaching methods, and educational innovations. Readers will discover strategies for stimulating students' creativity, fostering critical thinking skills, and encouraging innovative approaches to learning. Practical examples and case studies will showcase how educators have embraced creativity to enhance the learning experience and prepare students for future challenges.

Creative Problem-Solving in Technology

Technology is an ever-expanding field that thrives on creative problem-solving. This subsection will explore how creativity can be harnessed to drive technological advancements, design user-friendly interfaces, and solve complex technological challenges. Readers will learn about innovative technical problem-solving approaches like user-centred design, agile methodologies, and prototyping. Practical examples and case studies will highlight how technology companies have leveraged creative problem-solving to develop groundbreaking products, improve user experiences, and push the boundaries of innovation.

Creative Problem-Solving in Healthcare

The healthcare industry has unique issues that necessitate innovative problem-solving techniques. This subsection will explore how creativity can be applied in healthcare settings to address patient care, medical research, and healthcare management. Readers will discover innovative solutions developed to improve patient outcomes, enhance healthcare delivery, and streamline processes within healthcare organizations. Practical examples and case studies will showcase how creative problem-solving has transformed healthcare practices, from implementing new treatment approaches to designing patient-centered healthcare systems.

Creative Problem-Solving in Social and Environmental Issues

Solving societal challenges and addressing environmental issues requires a creative and innovative mindset. This subsection will explore how creative problem-solving techniques can be applied to tackle social and ecological problems. Readers will learn about innovative approaches to community development, sustainability, and social entrepreneurship. We will explore methods for identifying creative solutions, engaging stakeholders, and implementing impactful initiatives. Through practical examples and case studies, readers will learn how creative problem-solving can drive positive change and impact society.

Takeaway for the Chapter:

In Chapter 6, we have explored the power of creativity and innovation in problem-solving. From cultivating creative thinking skills to overcoming creative blocks and applying innovative problem-solving techniques to specific domains, readers have gained valuable insights into unleashing their creative potential and approaching challenges with fresh perspectives. They have learned how creativity can be applied in business, education, technology, healthcare, and social and environmental issues. By embracing creativity and fostering an innovative mindset, readers will be better equipped to tackle complex problems, drive innovation, and make a positive impact in their chosen domains.

Introduction to the Next Chapter: Chapter 7 - Collaboration and Communication

Building upon the foundation of creative problem-solving, Chapter 7 will focus on the importance of collaboration and communication in problem-solving endeavors. We will explore collaborative problem-solving techniques, effective communication strategies, and the power of collective intelligence in finding innovative solutions. Readers will discover how to harness the strengths of diverse teams, overcome communication barriers, and foster a collaborative culture. Join us in Chapter 7 as we unlock the potential of collaboration and communication in mastering the art of critical thinking, reasoning, and problem-solving.

CHAPTER SEVEN
COLLABORATION AND COMMUNICATION

Collaborative problem-solving techniques are essential for effective teamwork and successful problem resolution. We will look at numerous tactics in this part and methods that promote collaboration among team members and enhance problem-solving.

Collaborative problem-solving involves pooling together team members' knowledge, skills, and perspectives to analyze problems, generate ideas, and develop solutions collectively. By engaging in collaborative problem-solving, individuals can benefit from the diverse expertise and experiences of the team, leading to more robust and innovative solutions.

One key aspect of collaborative problem-solving is creating an environment that encourages open communication and active participation. Team members should feel free to express their ideas, thoughts, and concerns without fear of being judged or criticized. Establishing psychological safety within the group is crucial to foster a collaborative mindset.

Effective communication plays a vital role in collaborative problem-solving. Team members must be able to express their ideas clearly, actively listen to others, and engage in constructive discussions. Active listening involves paying attention to the perspectives of others, seeking clarification when needed, and demonstrating empathy. It allows team members to understand different viewpoints, identify common ground, and build upon each other's ideas.

Collaborative problem-solving techniques often involve structured processes and frameworks that guide the team through the problem-solving journey. These techniques can include brainstorming, where team members generate many ideas without judgment and then refine and evaluate them collectively. Another method uses visual tools such as mind maps or concept maps to represent and connect ideas visually. These tools help organize thoughts, identify relationships between concepts, and stimulate creativity.

Collaborative problem-solving also benefits from effective task distribution and role allocation within the team. Each team member can contribute their expertise and talents to problem solutions. By distributing work and responsibilities based on individual skills and interests, teams can optimize their collaborative efforts and ensure that all perspectives are considered.

In addition to these techniques, fostering a culture of trust and respect within the team is essential. Trust enables team members to freely express their opinions, take risks, and learn from failures. Respectful communication ensures that all team members feel valued and heard, regardless of their position or background.

By incorporating collaborative problem-solving techniques into the problem-solving process, teams can tap into their members' collective intelligence and creativity. They can generate a broader range of ideas, consider diverse perspectives, and make more informed decisions. Through effective collaboration and communication, teams can overcome challenges, leverage their collective strengths, and achieve successful problem resolution.

Effective Communication Strategies for Collaborative Problem-Solving

Effective communication is a cornerstone of successful collaborative problem-solving. This section will explore various strategies and techniques that facilitate clear and efficient communication within a team.

Active Listening: Active listening focuses

entirely on and comprehends what others say. It requires giving undivided attention, asking clarifying questions, and summarizing key points to ensure accurate understanding. Active listening promotes a shared understanding of the problem and fosters effective collaboration.

Clear and Concise Communication: Communicating ideas and solutions clearly and concisely is crucial for effective collaboration. Using simple language helps avoid confusion and ensures that everyone on the team understands the shared information. Additionally, organizing thoughts logically and presenting structured information helps convey ideas more effectively.

Respectful Communication: Maintaining a respectful communication environment is vital for fostering collaboration. Team members should express their opinions and provide feedback in a constructive and supportive manner. Respectful communication promotes open dialogue, encourages diverse perspectives, and creates a positive team dynamic.

Effective Feedback: Providing and receiving feedback is essential to collaborative problem-solving. Constructive feedback helps team members improve their ideas and solutions by highlighting strengths and areas for improvement. By offering feedback respectfully and constructively, team members can contribute to the growth and development of the entire team.

Non-Verbal Communication: Body language and tone of voice greatly influence nonverbal cues such as facial expressions. Being aware of non-verbal cues and using them effectively can enhance understanding and strengthen team dynamics. Non-verbal communication can convey emotions, attitudes, and intentions, influencing collaborative problem-solving.

Building Trust and Psychological Safety: Trust is the foundation of effective collaboration. Team members must feel comfortable sharing their ideas, taking risks, and expressing their concerns without fear of judgment or reprisal. Fostering a sense of psychological safety within the team encourages open and honest communication, enabling members to contribute fully and engage in productive problem-solving.

Utilizing Technology Tools: In today's digital age, technology offers numerous communication tools that facilitate collaboration among team members, even when geographically dispersed. Platforms like video conferencing, instant messaging, and project management software enable real-time communication, file sharing, and collaborative document editing. Leveraging these tools effectively can enhance communication and streamline the collaborative problem-solving process.

Case Studies and Interactive Activities: This section will include case studies and interactive activities to provide practical insights into effective communication strategies for collaborative problem-solving. Readers will have the opportunity to analyze real-world scenarios, identify communication challenges, and propose solutions. By engaging in these activities, readers can apply the communication strategies discussed and develop collaborative problem-solving skills.

The following section will explore team dynamics and the factors contributing to successful collaboration. We will delve into the roles and responsibilities within a team, team-building strategies, and the importance of effective leadership in driving collaborative problem-solving.

Engaging Readers through Group Activities and Case Studies

This section will incorporate group activities and case studies to enhance reader engagement and provide a practical application of collaborative problem-solving techniques. By actively participating in group activities, readers can apply the concepts and strategies discussed in real-life scenarios. These activities can include group discussions, problem-solving simulations, role-playing exercises, and collaborative projects.

Group activities encourage readers to collaborate, share ideas, and collectively develop solutions to complex problems. They foster teamwork, communication, and critical thinking skills, allowing readers to experience the challenges and rewards of collaborative problem-solving firsthand. Through these activities, readers can better understand the dynamics of working collaboratively and gain insights into practical strategies for overcoming obstacles and achieving successful outcomes.

In addition to group activities, case studies will showcase real-world examples of collaborative problem-solving. These case studies will highlight the challenges teams face, the strategies to overcome them, and the outcomes achieved through effective collaboration. By analyzing these case studies, readers can gain valuable insights into the practical application of collaborative problem-solving techniques across various domains and industries.

Furthermore, interactive exercises and discussions will be incorporated to encourage readers to reflect on their own experiences with collaborative problem-solving and share their insights and learnings. Through these interactive elements, readers can engage with the content on a deeper level, exchange ideas and perspectives, and further enhance their understanding and application of collaborative problem-solving concepts.

The combination of group activities, case studies, and interactive exercises ensures that readers are actively involved in the learning process, enabling them to internalize the principles of collaborative problem-solving and develop the necessary skills to work in teams and achieve collective goals effectively.

BUILDING TRUST AND RESOLVING CONFLICTS IN COLLABORATIVE SETTINGS

Embracing Diversity and Inclusion in Collaborative Problem-Solving:
Diversity in perspectives, backgrounds, and experiences can significantly enrich collaborative problem-solving. This section will emphasize embracing diversity and promoting inclusion within teams. Readers will learn strategies for fostering an inclusive environment that values and leverages the unique contributions of each team member. We will explore techniques for active participation and equal representation, ensuring that diverse voices are heard and respected. By embracing diversity and inclusion, teams can tap into various insights and ideas, leading to more innovative and effective problem-solving

outcomes.

Effective Decision-Making in Collaborative Settings:

Collaborative problem-solving often involves making decisions as a team. In this section, we will delve into the process of effective decision-making within collaborative settings. Readers will learn about decision-making models, techniques for reaching consensus, and approaches for balancing individual perspectives and collective goals. We will explore strategies for evaluating options, considering risks and benefits, and making informed decisions aligning with the team's objectives. By understanding the dynamics of decision-making in collaborative settings, readers will enhance their ability to contribute to decision-making and make sound choices as part of a team.

Measuring and Evaluating Collaborative Problem-Solving Effectiveness:

In this part, we'll talk about how crucial it is to gauge and assess the success of group problem-solving initiatives. Readers will learn about key performance indicators (KPIs) and metrics that can be used to determine the success and impact of joint problem-solving initiatives. We will explore techniques for gathering feedback, analyzing data, and making data-driven improvements to enhance the collaborative problem-solving process. By incorporating measurement and evaluation practices, teams can continuously learn and adapt, improving their problem-solving abilities.

LEVERAGING TECHNOLOGY FOR COLLABORATIVE PROBLEM-SOLVING

Technology is crucial in facilitating collaboration and problem-solving in today's digital age. This subtopic will explore how technology can be leveraged to enhance collaborative problem-solving efforts. We will discuss various digital tools and platforms that enable remote collaboration, real-time communication (Howe, J. (2008). Crowdsourcing: Why the Power of the Crowd Is Driving the Future of Business.), and document sharing. Readers will learn how to utilize project management software, collaborative whiteboards, video conferencing tools, and other technological resources to streamline communication, coordinate tasks, and facilitate collaboration among team members, even when geographically dispersed. **Howe, J. (2008). Crowdsourcing: Why the Power of the Crowd Is Driving the Future of Business.**

Virtual Collaboration: Overcoming the Challenges of Remote Collaboration:
With the increasing prevalence of remote work and distributed teams, virtual collaboration has become vital to problem-solving. This subtopic will address the unique challenges and considerations associated with remote collaboration. Readers will

124

gain insights into strategies for effective virtual communication, establishing clear communication channels, managing time zones, and fostering a sense of connection and engagement among remote team members. We will explore techniques for maintaining productivity, organizing virtual meetings, and utilizing collaborative software to bridge the physical distance and achieve effective collaboration.

Data Analytics and Decision Support Systems:

Data analytics and decision support systems provide valuable insights and support in collaborative problem-solving. This subtopic will explore how data analytics tools and techniques can analyze large datasets, identify patterns, and make data-driven decisions. Readers will learn about decision support systems that assist in complex decision-making processes by providing relevant information, visualizations, and predictive modelling. By leveraging data analytics and decision support systems, teams can enhance their problem-solving capabilities, uncover hidden insights, and make more informed decisions.

Ethics and Social Responsibility in Collaborative Problem-Solving:

Collaborative problem-solving extends beyond achieving solutions; it also involves considering the ethical and social implications of the decisions made.

This subtopic will explore ethical considerations and social responsibility Readers will explore the ethical frameworks and principles that guide decision-making in a collaborative setting. We'll talk about how crucial it is to think about how solutions will affect communities, stakeholders, and the environment. By integrating ethical and social responsibility considerations into collaborative problem-solving, teams can ensure their answers align with ethical standards and contribute positively to society.

GROUP ACTIVITIES AND CASE STUDIES

Group activities and case studies provide valuable opportunities for readers to engage in collaborative problem-solving and gain practical insights into real-world scenarios. This subtopic will explore the benefits of group activities and case studies as learning tools for developing problem-solving skills.

Interactive Group Activities:

Group activities encourage active participation and collaboration among readers. These activities can take various forms, such as group discussions, brainstorming sessions, role-playing exercises, and problem-solving simulations. By working together in a group setting, readers can learn from different perspectives, exchange ideas, and collectively find innovative solutions to complex problems. Group activities foster teamwork, communication, and critical thinking skills for effective collaborative problem-solving.

Case Studies:
Case studies give readers examples and problems they must solve in the current world. These scenarios can be drawn from various domains such as business, education, technology, healthcare, and social issues. By analyzing and discussing case studies, readers can apply the problem-solving strategies and techniques they have learned in previous chapters to practical situations. Case studies also help readers develop critical evaluation skills as they learn to analyze information, identify key issues, and make informed decisions based on the available data.

Benefits of Group Activities and Case Studies:
Engaging readers in group activities and case studies offer several benefits. Firstly, it promotes active learning and a deeper understanding of problem-solving concepts by providing hands-on experiences. Readers can apply theoretical knowledge to real-world contexts, enhancing their problem-solving skills and confidence. Secondly, group activities and case studies foster collaboration and teamwork, allowing readers to learn from each other's perspectives and collectively tackle complex challenges. This collaborative learning environment stimulates critical thinking and encourages the

exploration of diverse ideas and solutions. Lastly, group activities and case studies bridge theory and practice, enabling readers to see the practical application of problem-solving strategies and frameworks in different contexts.

ENHANCING VIRTUAL COLLABORATION AND COMMUNICATION

Virtual collaboration has become increasingly common in today's digital age, especially with remote work and online collaboration tools. This section will focus on strategies and techniques for enhancing virtual collaboration and communication, enabling individuals and teams to collaborate effectively despite geographical and technological barriers.

Utilizing Virtual Collaboration Tools:

We will explore various virtual collaboration tools and platforms that facilitate communication and collaboration in remote settings. This may include project management software, video conferencing platforms, shared document repositories, and instant messaging tools. Readers will learn to leverage these tools effectively to enhance communication, streamline workflows, and foster collaboration in virtual environments.

Establishing Clear Communication Channels:

Clear communication is crucial for virtual

collaboration. This subtopic will discuss the importance of establishing clear communication channels like email, chat, video conferencing, and virtual meetings. Readers will learn strategies for effective virtual communication, including using concise and specific language, active listening, and the importance of regular check-ins and updates.

Building Trust and Connection in Virtual Teams:
Building trust and connecting with virtual team members is essential for successful collaboration. We will explore techniques for building trust in virtual teams, such as creating opportunities for informal interactions, promoting transparency, and recognizing and valuing individual contributions. Readers will gain insights into virtual team dynamics and learn strategies for promoting a collaborative and supportive virtual environment.

Overcoming Challenges in Virtual Collaboration:
Virtual collaboration presents unique challenges, such as time zone differences, language barriers, and technological issues. This subtopic will address these challenges and provide strategies for overcoming them. Readers will learn to manage and adapt to different time zones, enhance cross-cultural communication, and troubleshoot common technological issues to ensure smooth collaboration and effective problem-solving.

Engaging in Virtual Collaboration Activities:

To enhance the learning experience, this section will include engaging virtual collaboration activities. These activities will encourage readers to participate in virtual problem-solving scenarios, team project activity, and discussions using virtual collaboration tools. By experiencing virtual collaboration's challenges and benefits firsthand, readers will gain practical skills and insights into effective virtual collaboration.

By exploring the strategies and techniques for enhancing virtual collaboration and communication, readers will be equipped with the knowledge and skills to collaborate in virtual environments effectively. They will learn to utilize virtual collaboration tools, establish clear communication channels, build trust in virtual teams, overcome challenges, and engage in productive virtual collaboration activities.

TAKEAWAY

This chapter explored the importance of collaboration and effective communication in problem-solving. We learned about collaborative problem-solving techniques, the significance of building trust and resolving conflicts in team settings, and the role of technology in facilitating collaboration. Through group activities, case studies, and discussions on virtual collaboration, readers gained practical insights into fostering collaboration, communicating ideas effectively, and leveraging technology for productive teamwork. By developing strong collaboration and communication skills, readers are better equipped to tackle complex problems and achieve successful outcomes.

Introducing Chapter 8

As we move forward in our journey of mastering critical thinking and problem-solving, Chapter 8 dives into ethical and moral reasoning. This chapter explores the principles and frameworks that guide our ethical decision-making processes. We delve into discussions on moral values, ethical dilemmas, and the ethical implications of our actions. Through thought-provoking examples and real-world scenarios, we invite readers to engage in ethical reasoning and reflect on the impact of their choices. Join us as we navigate the complexities of ethical and moral reasoning, and discover how these principles can shape our problem-solving approaches for the better.

CHAPTER EIGHT
ETHICAL AND MORAL REASONING

In this pivotal chapter, we embark on a journey into the realm of ethical and moral reasoning, illuminating its vital role in critical thinking and problem-solving. By exploring how ethical considerations intertwine with decision-making and problem-solving, we equip our readers with invaluable tools and frameworks to navigate complex ethical dilemmas, make well-informed, ethical decisions, and evaluate the profound moral implications of their choices.

Drawing upon the rich insights from Velasquez, M., Andre, C., Shanks, T., and Meyer, M. J. (2019), "Thinking Ethically: A Framework for Moral Decision Making," we delve into a systematic approach to ethical reasoning that empowers readers to think critically and make sound moral judgments. This renowned text provides a comprehensive framework that combines ethical theories with practical applications, enabling individuals to navigate the intricate landscape of ethical decision-making.

Through interactive exercises and thought-provoking discussions, this chapter aims to foster a deep understanding of ethical reasoning and highlight its importance in critical thinking. We recognize that moral reasoning is not merely an abstract concept but a guiding compass that shapes our actions and character. By delving into this topic, we provide readers with the necessary skills to navigate the intricate landscape of ethical dilemmas and make choices that align with their values and principles.

As we embark on this exploration, we invite readers to engage actively with the content, reflecting on their ethical frameworks and critically examining the moral dimensions of real-world scenarios. By immersing themselves in the rich tapestry of ethical reasoning, readers will broaden their intellectual horizons and develop a heightened sense of moral responsibility in their personal and professional lives.

So, let us embark on this transformative chapter together as we delve into the depths of ethical and moral reasoning, empowering ourselves to become astute critical thinkers capable of making ethical decisions that shape a better future.

Ethical Considerations in Critical Thinking and Problem-Solving

Ethical considerations play a vital role in critical thinking and problem-solving. They provide a moral compass that guides our choices and actions, ensuring that we align with principles and values essential to us as individuals and as a society. In this section, we delve into the significance of ethics in the decision-making process and how it enhances the quality and integrity of our problem-solving approach.

One aspect we explore is ethical theories, which offer frameworks for assessing the ethical implications of our decisions. These theories, such as consequentialism, deontology, and virtue ethics, provide different perspectives on what is morally right or wrong and help us evaluate the potential consequences of our actions. By understanding these ethical theories, readers can better understand the moral landscape and make more informed and ethically sound decisions.

Furthermore, we discuss ethical principles and frameworks that can be used in problem-solving and critical thinking. These principles, such as fairness, integrity, and respect for autonomy, guide navigating ethical challenges and dilemmas. Incorporating these principles into our decision-making process ensures that our solutions are practical and ethically responsible.

By considering ethical considerations in critical thinking, readers develop a more comprehensive approach to problem-solving. They learn to examine the potential ethical implications of their actions, evaluate the trade-offs between different stakeholders' interests, and consider the long-term consequences of their decisions. Considering the broader moral context, this holistic perspective allows for a more balanced and responsible problem-solving process.

In summary, understanding and integrating ethical considerations in critical thinking and problem-solving enable us to make choices that are not only effective but also morally grounded. By exploring ethical theories, principles, and frameworks, readers gain the tools to assess the ethical implications of their decisions and navigate complex ethical challenges. This ethical lens enhances the quality and integrity of our problem-solving approach, ensuring that our solutions align with our values and contribute to a better and more open world. (Melden, 1955)

Addressing Moral Dilemmas and Ethical Decision-Making

Moral dilemmas present individuals with difficult choices where no option seems completely satisfactory and where adhering to one ethical principle may conflict with another. Addressing moral dilemmas requires a thoughtful and reflective approach to ethical decision-making. This section explores strategies for navigating these challenging situations and making informed ethical choices.

Firstly, we will discuss the importance of analyzing moral dilemmas from multiple perspectives. Understanding the various ethical considerations helps us comprehensively appreciate the situation's complexity. By examining the potential consequences, stakeholders involved, and underlying values, readers develop a deeper appreciation for the intricacies of moral dilemmas.

Next, we will delve into evaluating potential solutions to moral dilemmas. We explore ethical frameworks and decision-making models that can guide our analysis and help us weigh the competing ethical principles at stake. By considering the implications of each alternative and evaluating them against ethical standards, readers' decisions will be more in line with their ideals.

Real-world case studies and examples are incorporated to provide practical insights into navigating moral dilemmas. By examining how others have approached similar situations, readers can gain valuable perspectives and learn from their experiences. These case studies highlight the complexities of ethical decision-making and demonstrate the importance of thoughtful reflection and moral reasoning.

Furthermore, we will emphasize the significance of balancing competing ethical principles when addressing moral dilemmas. Ethical decision-making often involves trade-offs between different values and interests. By recognizing and acknowledging these conflicts, readers can strive to find a middle ground that maximizes ethical considerations and minimizes harm.

This section includes interactive exercises and discussions to engage readers in analyzing ethical scenarios and discussing potential solutions. These activities allow readers to apply their ethical reasoning skills, consider different perspectives, and engage in critical dialogue. By actively participating in these exercises, readers enhance their ability to navigate moral dilemmas and make ethical decisions in real-world situations.

In summary, addressing moral dilemmas and engaging in ethical decision-making requires a thoughtful and reflective approach. Readers can make informed choices that align with their values by analyzing moral dilemmas, evaluating potential solutions, and considering competing ethical principles. Through case studies and interactive activities, readers develop their ethical reasoning skills and gain practical insights into navigating complex ethical challenges.

Interactive Exercises: Analyzing Ethical Scenarios and Discussing Potential Solutions

Interactive exercises are crucial in engaging readers and providing them with practical application of ethical reasoning skills. In this section on analyzing ethical scenarios and discussing potential solutions, readers will actively participate in exercises that simulate real-life ethical dilemmas. These interactive activities immerse readers in ethical decision-making and foster a deeper understanding of the complexities involved.

The interactive exercises begin by presenting readers with ethical scenarios that involve conflicting values, principles, or interests. These scenarios may affect challenging ethical dilemmas in various contexts, such as healthcare, business, or personal relationships. Readers are encouraged to analyze the strategies from multiple perspectives, considering the potential consequences, stakeholders involved, and underlying ethical considerations.

As readers engage in the exercises, they will be prompted to critically evaluate the ethical implications of each scenario and propose potential solutions. They will be encouraged to think deeply about the moral principles at stake and consider how different courses of action may impact various individuals or groups. Through this process, readers develop their ethical reasoning skills, learning to navigate complex moral dilemmas and make informed decisions.

Moreover, the interactive exercises will promote discussion and collaboration among readers. Group activities are incorporated, allowing readers to engage in dialogue, share their perspectives, and debate the merits of different ethical solutions. Through these discussions, readers gain exposure to diverse viewpoints and learn to appreciate the complexity of ethical decision-making.

The exercises will encourage readers to reflect on their ethical values and beliefs. By confronting challenging ethical scenarios and discussing potential solutions, readers are prompted to examine their moral compass and evaluate the consistency between their values and their proposed actions. This self-reflection fosters personal growth and a deeper understanding of ethical principles.

The interactive nature of these exercises provides readers with a hands-on learning experience, enabling them to actively apply ethical reasoning skills and gain practical insights into ethical decision-making. By engaging in these activities, readers develop critical thinking skills, empathy, and a greater appreciation for the moral complexities that arise in various situations.

Throughout the exercises, readers are guided by thought-provoking questions, prompts, and guidelines to help structure their analysis and discussions. This ensures that the interactive activities provide a supportive learning environment that encourages a thoughtful exploration of ethical scenarios and considering diverse perspectives.

In conclusion, the interactive exercises in this section on analyzing ethical scenarios and discussing potential solutions are designed to actively engage readers in moral reasoning and decision-making. By immersing themselves in realistic ethical dilemmas, readers develop their ethical reasoning skills, gain practical insights into ethical decision-making, and learn to appreciate the complexity of ethical considerations. Through group discussions and reflection, readers deepen their understanding of their moral values and enhance their ability to navigate real-life ethical challenges.

TAKEAWAY

Chapter 8 highlights the importance of ethical and moral reasoning in critical thinking and problem-solving. By integrating ethical considerations into decision-making, readers can navigate moral dilemmas, make informed choices, and uphold ethical principles. Through interactive exercises and real-world examples, readers gain practical experience analyzing ethical scenarios and discussing potential solutions. The appendices provide additional resources and tools to further support readers in developing their moral reasoning skills.

Chapter 9 focuses on the crucial skills of adaptability and resilience in critical thinking and problem-solving. In an ever-changing and uncertain world, these skills are vital for success. Readers will learn strategies for building strength and developing a mindset that embraces change and uncertainty. The chapter explores techniques for effectively navigating complexity, including scenario planning, iterative problem-solving, and seeking diverse perspectives. Additionally, readers will be introduced to online resources and interactive tools that can enhance their problem-solving abilities and provide ongoing support.

Join us in Chapter 9 as we explore how to adapt to uncertainty and change, building the skills necessary to thrive in dynamic environments.

CHAPTER NINE
ADAPTING TO UNCERTAINTY
AND CHANGE

Adapting to uncertainty in today's rapidly changing and unpredictable world is crucial for practical critical thinking and problem-solving. This chapter will explore the concept of resilience and its role in navigating uncertainty and complexity. Readers will learn strategies and techniques for building resilience in their problem-solving approach, enabling them to thrive in dynamic and unpredictable environments.

Strategies for Navigating Uncertainty and Complexity:
Uncertainty and complexity are inherent aspects of problem-solving in today's fast-paced and dynamic world. This section will explore strategies for navigating uncertainty and complexity in critical thinking and problem-solving processes. Readers will learn techniques for analyzing complex problems, managing ambiguity, and adapting their approaches when faced with uncertain

circumstances. We will discuss the importance of embracing a growth mindset, remaining flexible in the face of change, and utilizing problem-solving frameworks adaptable to different situations. By developing these strategies, readers will become more adept at handling uncertainty and complexity, leading to more effective problem-solving outcomes.

Online Resources and Interactive Tools for Practice and Support:

In the digital age, many online resources and interactive tools are available to support critical thinking and problem-solving. This section will introduce readers to various online platforms, websites, and tools that can enhance their problem-solving skills. These resources may include interactive problem-solving simulations, online courses, educational websites, and digital libraries. Readers will learn how to leverage these resources to practice and refine their critical thinking abilities, access additional learning materials, and connect with communities of problem solvers. By utilizing online resources and interactive tools, readers can develop their problem-solving capabilities and stay updated with the latest insights and techniques.

Ethical Decision-Making in Critical Thinking and Problem-Solving

Ethical considerations are integral to critical thinking and problem-solving, guiding individuals to make morally sound decisions aligned with moral principles. This chapter will explore ethical decision-making and its significance in addressing complex problems. Readers will gain insights into ethical theories, examine real-world case studies, and engage in interactive exercises to sharpen their moral reasoning skills.

Analyzing Ethical Dilemmas and Complex Scenarios:
Ethical dilemmas often present complex situations where competing values and moral obligations are at play. This section will explore strategies for analyzing and evaluating ethical dilemmas and complex scenarios. Readers will learn how to identify the stakeholders involved, assess the potential consequences of different actions, and consider the ethical principles and values at stake. By examining case studies and real-world examples, readers will develop their ability to analyze ethical dilemmas and make well-reasoned decisions critically. They will also gain insight into the complexities and nuances involved in ethical decision-making.

Ethical decision-making is a skill that can be developed through practice and reflection. This section will discuss practical steps and strategies for enhancing ethical decision-making skills. Readers will learn techniques such as moral reasoning, ethical thinking, and considering alternative perspectives. We will also explore the role of empathy and moral imagination in understanding the impact of decisions on others. By actively engaging in ethical decision-making exercises and reflecting on their values and principles, readers will strengthen their ability to make ethically sound choices in various contexts.

Promoting Ethical Behavior and Responsible Problem-Solving:

Ethical behavior and responsible problem-solving go hand in hand. This section will examine strategies for promoting ethical conduct in critical thinking and problem-solving processes. Readers will explore the importance of integrity, transparency, and accountability in decision-making. We'll also discuss the significance of leadership and organizational culture in supporting ethical behavior. By aligning their actions with ethical principles and promoting ethical behavior within their spheres of influence, readers will contribute to a culture of responsible problem-solving and ethical decision-making.

CHAPTER TEN
CONCLUDING THOUGHTS

Transformative Power of Mastering Critical Thinking and Problem-Solving

Restating the Message of the Book Using New Language:

As we bid farewell to this enlightening expedition, let us reiterate the book's core message in a new light. Throughout our odyssey, we have unveiled the immense value of cultivating critical thinking, reasoning, and problem-solving skills. By embracing these cognitive tools, we empower ourselves to analyze complex information, make informed decisions, overcome challenges, and forge innovative solutions. Mastering these skills unlocks a world of possibilities, propelling us towards personal and professional growth while contributing to a brighter future for ourselves and society.

Summarizing the Most Important Topics Covered:

Throughout our journey, we have discovered that

mastering critical thinking, reasoning, and problem-solving is not merely theoretical but a practical and transformative endeavor. We have witnessed the profound impact these skills can have on our personal growth, professional success, and the betterment of society.

Critical thinking has empowered us to question assumptions, challenge biases, and think critically about the information presented. It has allowed us to analyze complex issues, evaluate evidence, and make informed decisions based on logic and reason. We have learned to separate fact from fiction, recognize logical fallacies, and approach arguments with skepticism and open-mindedness.

In problem-solving, we have become adept at breaking down problems into manageable parts, identifying root causes, and generating creative and innovative solutions. We have embraced the power of brainstorming, lateral thinking, and collaboration to unlock new perspectives and approaches. Our problem-solving skills have allowed us to tackle challenges confidently and continuously, overcoming obstacles and finding pathways to success.

Creativity has emerged as an essential companion on our journey, encouraging us to think beyond the boundaries of tradition and explore unconventional ideas. We have learned brainstorming, mind mapping, and free association techniques to ignite our imagination and foster divergent thinking. Embracing creativity has liberated us from the constraints of linear thinking and enabled us to find unique and innovative solutions to complex problems.

Collaboration and effective communication have proven to be essential skills in our toolkit. We have come to appreciate the power of diverse perspectives and the collective intelligence of teams. By working together, we have unlocked synergies, leveraged individual strengths, and achieved outcomes surpassing what anyone could accomplish alone. Effective communication has allowed us to articulate our ideas, listen attentively to others, and foster understanding and cooperation.

Ethical and moral reasoning have guided us in making principled decisions and considering the broader impact of our actions. We have explored ethical theories and principles, recognizing the importance of autonomy, justice, and beneficence in our decision-making. By integrating ethical considerations into our thinking process, we have become agents of positive change, advocating for fairness, compassion, and societal well-being.

In a world characterized by uncertainty and change, we have developed resilience. We have learned to adapt, embrace ambiguity, and view challenges as opportunities for growth. Resilience has equipped us with the strength and flexibility to navigate the ever-evolving landscape with confidence and determination. We have embraced the mindset of lifelong learning, continuously seeking new knowledge and skills to stay agile and relevant.

As we conclude our journey, let us carry these lessons, insights, and strategies. Let us continue to cultivate our critical thinking skills, nurture our creativity, collaborate with others, and make ethical decisions that shape a better world. The power to think critically, reason effectively, and solve problems creatively is within each of us. It is a power that can transform not only our own lives but also the lives of those around us.

So, as you venture beyond these pages, remember the transformative potential within you. Embrace the challenges that come your way, for they are opportunities for growth and learning. Trust in your ability to analyze, evaluate, and solve problems. Be open to new ideas, perspectives, and possibilities. And above all, I have the confidence to be a catalyst for positive change, utilizing the power of critical thinking, reasoning, and problem-solving to create a brighter, more promising future for all.

The journey does not end here; it is a lifelong pursuit. May you continue to develop and sharpen your critical thinking skills because they are the compass that will lead you to success.

Recap of Key Concepts and Strategies Learned Throughout the Book:

As we reflect on our shared exploration, let us recall the key concepts and strategies that have enriched our understanding and sharpened our skills:

Critical thinking is the foundation for informed decision-making and problem-solving.

Problem-solving frameworks, including the scientific method, root cause analysis, design thinking, and decision-making frameworks such as cost-benefit analysis and SWOT analysis.

We cultivate creativity through brainstorming, mind mapping, and embracing unconventional approaches.

Collaboration and effective communication are essential for successful problem-solving in a team setting.

Ethical and moral reasoning to navigate complex ethical dilemmas and make conscientious decisions.

It is building resilience to adapt to uncertainty and change, fostering a positive mindset in the face of challenges.

Encouragement for Readers to Continue Developing Their Critical Thinking Skills:

To our esteemed readers, we extend our heartfelt encouragement to persist in growth and development in critical thinking, reasoning, and problem-solving. Remember that mastery in these areas is not achieved through a single journey but through a lifetime commitment to learning and refinement. Seek opportunities to apply these skills in your personal and professional life, embrace intellectual challenges, and actively seek feedback to deepen your understanding and hone your abilities. Engage with others who share a passion for critical thinking, fostering a community of learning and support. Embracing a continuous growth mindset will unlock your full potential and catalyze positive change.

Key Takeaway for the Reader:

In our exploration of critical thinking, reasoning, and problem-solving, we have witnessed the profound impact these skills can have on our lives. They empower us to make informed decisions, unravel complex issues, and adapt to the ever-changing world with resilience. But let us not forget that the true power of these skills lies in their application and continual development and refinement.

As you embark on your continued journey, remember to seek opportunities for growth and learning. Embrace intellectual curiosity and approach every challenge as an opportunity for growth. Surround yourself with people who share your enthusiasm for critical thinking and engage in philosophical debates that question your assumptions. Explore new disciplines, delve into diverse sources of knowledge, and be open to new ideas that expand your understanding.

Remember that progress may not always be linear in mastering critical thinking, reasoning, and problem-solving. There will be setbacks and moments of uncertainty. But it is in these moments that your resilience and determination will shine through. Embrace the challenges as opportunities to learn and improve. Reflect on your experiences, celebrate successes, and learn from failures. With each step, you will build a solid foundation of skills and knowledge that will propel you forward.

As you navigate your personal and professional endeavors, Put the principles and tactics you've studied to use. Continually evaluate your thinking, challenge assumptions, and seek multiple perspectives. Embrace diversity and actively listen to the ideas and opinions of others. By doing so, you will cultivate a well-rounded understanding of the world and develop the ability to find innovative solutions to complex problems.

Remember that the power of critical thinking,

reasoning, and problem-solving extends beyond the boundaries of your own life. Use your skills to make a positive impact in your community and society as a whole. Advocate for truth, justice, and ethical decision-making. Be a voice for unheard people and champion causes that promote equality, sustainability, and social well-being. By leveraging your skills, you have the potential to shape a better future for all.

As we part ways, I am grateful for accompanying me on this intellectual journey. Your commitment to personal growth and development is commendable, and I am confident that you will continue to thrive in mastering critical thinking, reasoning, and problem-solving. May your path be filled with curiosity, discovery, and meaningful contributions. Farewell, and may your journey be filled with endless possibilities and transformative experiences.

CONCLUSION

In conclusion, our journey through this book has explored the fundamental concepts, frameworks, and skills needed for practical critical thinking and problem-solving. We have examined the core elements of critical thinking, problem-solving methodologies, the role of creativity and collaboration, the significance of ethical reasoning, and the importance of resilience in adapting to uncertainty. As we reach the end of this book, we must reflect on the key insights and takeaways that will empower us in our pursuit of excellence in critical thinking and problem-solving. By internalizing the importance of critical thinking as a foundational skill, we can approach information and decision-making with a discerning eye, evaluating evidence and considering multiple perspectives. The systematic approach to problem-solving, incorporating methodologies such as root cause analysis and design thinking, equips us to break down complex challenges into manageable components and generate innovative solutions.

Furthermore, cultivating creativity allows us to think beyond conventional boundaries, fostering fresh perspectives and original ideas. Collaboration and effective communication emerge as essential tools in our problem-solving arsenal, leveraging teams' collective intelligence and diverse insights. Ethical and moral reasoning guides us in making principled decisions that align with our in conclusion, our journey through this book has explored the fundamental concepts, frameworks, and skills needed for practical critical thinking and problem-solving. We have examined the core elements of critical thinking, problem-solving methodologies, the role of creativity and collaboration, the significance of ethical reasoning, and the importance of resilience in adapting to uncertainty.

As we reach the end of this book, we must reflect on the key insights and takeaways that will empower us in our pursuit of excellence in critical thinking and problem-solving. By internalizing the importance of critical thinking as a foundational skill, we can approach information and decision-making with a discerning eye, evaluating evidence and considering multiple perspectives.

The systematic approach to problem-solving, incorporating methodologies such as root cause analysis and design thinking, equips us to break down complex challenges into manageable components and generate innovative solutions. Furthermore, cultivating creativity allows us to think beyond conventional boundaries, fostering fresh perspectives and original ideas.

Collaboration and effective communication emerge as essential tools in our problem-solving arsenal, leveraging teams' collective intelligence and diverse insights. Ethical and moral reasoning guides us in making principled decisions that align with our values and contribute to the greater good of society.

Adapting to uncertainty and change requires resilience, which enables us to bounce back from setbacks, maintain a positive mindset, and embrace new growth opportunities. By building strength, we become better equipped to navigate the dynamic landscape of our personal and professional lives.

As we conclude this book, we encourage you to continue developing critical thinking and problem-solving skills. Embrace a lifelong learning mindset, seeking opportunities to apply and refine your skills in real-world contexts. Engage in ongoing practice, seek feedback, and embrace challenges as opportunities for growth.

Becoming a proficient critical thinker and problem solver is a continuous journey. It requires dedication, persistence, and an insatiable curiosity to explore new ideas and possibilities. By honing these skills, you have the power to tackle complex problems, make informed decisions, and shape a better future.

We sincerely hope that this book has provided you with valuable insights, practical strategies, and inspiration to embark on this transformative journey of mastering critical thinking and problem-solving. May your endeavors be fruitful, and may your ability to think critically and solve problems positively impact your life and the lives of those around you.

Thank you for joining us on this enlightening expedition, and we wish you all the success in your ongoing pursuit of excellence in critical thinking and problem-solving. values and contribute to the greater good of society. Adapting to uncertainty and change requires resilience, which enables us to bounce back from setbacks, maintain a positive mindset, and embrace new growth opportunities. By building strength, we become better equipped to navigate the dynamic landscape of our personal and professional lives. As we conclude this book, we encourage you to continue developing critical thinking and problem-solving skills. Embrace a lifelong learning mindset, seeking opportunities to apply and refine your skills in real-world contexts. Engage in ongoing practice, seek feedback, and embrace challenges as opportunities for growth. Becoming a proficient critical thinker and problem solver is a continuous journey. It requires dedication, persistence, and an insatiable curiosity to explore new ideas and possibilities. By honing these skills, you have the power to tackle complex problems, make informed decisions, and shape a better future. We sincerely hope that this book has provided you with valuable insights, practical strategies, and inspiration to embark on this transformative journey of mastering critical thinking and problem-solving. May your endeavors be fruitful, and may your ability to think critically and solve problems positively impact your life and the lives of those around you. Thank you for joining us on this enlightening expedition, and we wish you all the success in your ongoing pursuit of excellence in critical thinking and problem-solving.

APPENDIX

This section of the book provides additional resources and materials to enhance your understanding and application of critical thinking and problem-solving skills. The appendices serve as valuable references, offering practical tools and examples that support your learning journey. Here are the appendices included in this book:

Additional Exercises and Practice Scenarios:
This appendix offers readers extra problem-solving exercises and scenarios specifically focused on critical thinking and problem-solving. These exercises provide opportunities for readers to further develop their skills and apply them to various situations.

Recommended Resources and Further Reading:
In this appendix, you will find a curated list of recommended resources and further reading materials. These resources cover a wide range of topics related to critical thinking, problem-solving,

creativity, collaboration, ethics, and more. They provide valuable insights and perspectives to deepen your knowledge in these areas.

Glossary of Key Terms:

The glossary contains definitions and explanations of key terms and concepts introduced throughout the book. It serves as a quick reference guide to clarify any terminology or jargon that may be encountered in the context of critical thinking and problem-solving.

Case Studies and Real-World Examples:

This appendix features a collection of case studies and real-world examples that illustrate the practical application of critical thinking and problem-solving skills. These case studies present scenarios from various fields, allowing you to analyze and discuss ethical dilemmas, creative solutions, and effective problem-solving strategies.

Online Resources and Interactive Tools:

This appendix provides a list of online resources and interactive tools that can further support your learning and practice. These resources may include websites, software applications, or online platforms that offer simulations, interactive exercises, and additional learning materials.

Critical Thinking Checklist and Templates:

This appendix offers a set of checklists and templates that can be used as practical tools for critical thinking and problem-solving. These resources provide a structured approach to guide your thinking process, ensuring that you consider all relevant factors and systematically evaluate options.

The appendices are designed to complement the main content of the book, providing you with supplementary materials and references to deepen your understanding and enhance your application of critical thinking and problem-solving skills. They offer opportunities for further exploration, practice, and reflection, supporting your continuous growth and development in these areas.

We encourage you to refer to the appendices as needed throughout your learning journey, utilizing the exercises, resources, and tools to reinforce your knowledge and skills. By engaging with these additional materials, you can further enhance your ability to think critically, solve problems effectively, and make informed decisions in various contexts.

RECOMMENDED RESOURCES AND FURTHER READING

In addition to the problem-solving exercises and scenarios, this appendix includes a curated list of recommended resources and further reading materials related to ethical and moral reasoning. These resources offer additional guidance, insights, and perspectives on ethical decision-making, moral philosophy, and applied ethics. Readers can explore these resources to deepen their knowledge, broaden their understanding of ethical principles, and stay updated on current ethical debates and discussions.

As we reflect on the entirety of this book, it is important to reiterate the key insights and takeaways that empower us in our pursuit of excellence in critical thinking and problem-solving.

Throughout this book, we have embarked on a comprehensive journey to develop and enhance our critical thinking and problem-solving skills. We have explored the foundational elements of critical thinking, including logical reasoning, analysis, and evaluation. We have examined various problem-solving frameworks and methodologies, providing a systematic approach to address challenges effectively.

Creativity has been a prominent theme, allowing us to think beyond traditional boundaries, generate innovative ideas, and approach problems with fresh perspectives. Collaboration and effective communication have been emphasized as essential tools in our problem-solving arsenal, enabling us to harness the collective intelligence and diverse insights of teams.

We have recognized the significance of ethical and moral reasoning in making principled decisions that align with our values and contribute to the greater good of society. Ethical considerations have guided our problem-solving efforts, ensuring that our actions are ethically responsible and have a positive impact.

Furthermore, we have acknowledged the importance of resilience in adapting to uncertainty and change. By building resilience, we can bounce back from setbacks, maintain a positive mindset, and embrace new growth opportunities. Resilience enables us to navigate the dynamic landscape of our personal and professional lives, ultimately contributing to our success in critical thinking and problem-solving.

As we conclude this book, we encourage you to continue your journey of development in critical thinking and problem-solving. Embrace a lifelong learning mindset, seek opportunities to apply and refine your skills, and engage in ongoing practice. Remember to seek feedback, embrace challenges, and continuously expand your knowledge and perspectives.

By honing your critical thinking and problem-solving skills, you have the power to tackle complex problems, make informed decisions, and shape a better future. Your ability to think critically and solve problems positively impacts not only your life but also the lives of those around you.

We sincerely hope that this book has provided you with valuable insights, practical strategies, and inspiration to embark on this transformative journey of mastering critical thinking and problem-solving. May your endeavors be fruitful, and may your ability to think critically and solve problems make a positive difference in the world.

Thank you for joining us on this enlightening expedition, and we wish you all the success in your ongoing pursuit of excellence in critical thinking and problem-solving.

CASE STUDIES AND REAL-WORLD EXAMPLES

These case studies and real-world examples serve as valuable learning tools, allowing readers to apply their ethical reasoning skills to concrete situations. Each case study presents a scenario that poses ethical challenges and dilemmas, requiring readers to analyze the situation, consider different perspectives, and propose potential solutions.

By engaging with these case studies, readers can develop a deeper understanding of the complexities involved in ethical decision-making. They will be challenged to think critically, weigh competing values, and navigate the ethical landscape. Through the examination of real-world examples, readers can broaden their knowledge of ethical considerations across a range of industries and professions.

Furthermore, the inclusion of case studies

encourages readers to explore the implications of ethical reasoning in their own lives and fields of interest. By studying how professionals have grappled with ethical dilemmas, readers can gain valuable insights and draw lessons that can be applied to their own decision-making processes.

In addition to the case studies, this appendix also presents real-world examples that showcase ethical reasoning in action. These examples highlight instances where individuals or organizations have faced ethical challenges and made decisions that align with ethical principles and values. By examining these examples, readers can gain a deeper appreciation for the practical application of ethical reasoning and understand the impact of ethical choices on individuals and society.

The inclusion of case studies and real-world examples in this appendix aims to enrich readers' understanding of ethical reasoning and decision-making. By examining these real-life scenarios, readers can enhance their ability to identify and address ethical dilemmas in their own lives and professions.

As you engage with these case studies and real-world examples, we encourage you to analyze the situations, consider the various stakeholders involved, and reflect on the ethical principles at play. Take the opportunity to discuss these examples with peers or mentors, fostering rich conversations that deepen your understanding of ethical reasoning.

By delving into these case studies and real-world examples, you will further develop your ethical reasoning skills, strengthen your ability to make principled decisions, and contribute to creating a more ethical and just society.

Please refer to the appendices section of this book for the full collection of case studies and real-world examples.

GLOSSARY OF KEY TERMS:

Throughout this book, we have introduced and discussed various vital critical thinking and problem-solving terms. To aid in your understanding and reference, here is a glossary of these essential terms:

- **Critical Thinking:** The active and skilled analysis procedure, evaluating, and synthesizing information to make reasoned judgments and decisions.

- **Problem-Solving:** Finding solutions to complex or challenging problems through systematic thinking, analysis, and evaluation.

- **Consequentialism:** An ethical theory that focuses on the consequences or outcomes of actions, emphasizing the most significant overall good or utility.

- **Deontology:** An ethical theory that emphasizes moral duties and principles, guiding actions based on the inherent nature of ethical rules.

- **Virtue Ethics:** An ethical theory that emphasizes the development of virtuous character traits and moral virtues as the basis for ethical behavior.

- **Autonomy:** The principle of respecting individuals' freedom and right to make decisions based on their values and beliefs.

- **Justice:** The principle of fairness and equal treatment, ensuring that individuals receive what is due to them and promoting equitable outcomes.

- **Beneficence:** The principle of doing good and promoting the well-being of others, often involving acts of kindness, compassion, and assistance.

- **Non-maleficence:** The principle of avoiding harm and preventing or minimizing potential damage to others.

- **Resilience:** The ability to bounce back from setbacks, adapt to change, and maintain a positive mindset.

- **Systematic Approach:** An organized and structured approach to problem-solving involving steps such as defining the problem, analyzing data, generating solutions, and evaluating outcomes.

- **Creativity:** The ability to generate original ideas, think outside the box, and approach problems from unconventional angles.

- **Collaboration:** Working together with others to achieve a common goal, leveraging diverse perspectives and skills for more effective problem-solving.

- **Communication:** The exchange of information, ideas, and thoughts between individuals or groups crucial for sharing insights, coordinating efforts, and fostering understanding.

- **Ethical Reasoning:** Applying ethical principles, values, and frameworks to analyze ethical dilemmas and make morally sound decisions.

- **Resilience:** The capacity to bounce back from challenges, adapt to change, and maintain a positive mindset in adversity.

This glossary serves as a reference to ensure a clear understanding of the key terms discussed throughout the book. It will help you navigate the concepts and discussions more effectively and deepen your comprehension of critical thinking and problem-solving principles.

RESOURCES

Dowden, B. H. (1993). *Logical Reasoning*. Bradley Dowden.

Dweck, C. S. (2006). Mindset: the new psychology of success. *Choice Reviews Online*, *44*(04), 44–2397. https://doi.org/10.5860/choice.44-2397

Gauch, H. G. (2003). *Scientific method in practice*. http://dx.doi.org/10.1017/cbo9780511815034

Van Aken, J. E., & Berends, H. (2018). *Problem-Solving in Organizations: A Methodological Handbook for Business and Management Students*. Cambridge University Press.

Weisberg, H. I. (2010). *Bias and Causation: Models and Judgment for Valid Comparisons*. Wiley.

Glantz, S. A., & Balbach, E. D. 2000). Tobacco war: Inside the California battles. University of California Press

Blyth, C. R. (1972). On Simpson's Paradox and the Sure-Thing Principle. *Journal of the American Statistical Association*, *67*(338), 364–366. https://doi.org/10.1080/01621459.1972.10482387

Pohl, R. F. (2012). Cognitive Illusions: A Handbook on Fallacies and Biases in Thinking, Judgement and Memory. Psychology Press.

Kahneman, D., Slovic, P., & Tversky, A. (1982). Judgment under Uncertainty: Heuristics and Biases. Cambridge University Press.

Kallet, M. (2014). Think Smarter: Critical Thinking to Improve Problem-Solving and Decision-Making Skills. John Wiley & Sons.

Pollastri, A. R., Ablon, J. S., & Hone, M. J. (2019). Collaborative Problem Solving: An Evidence-Based Approach to Implementation and Practice. Springer.

Howe, J. (2008). Crowdsourcing: Why the Power of the Crowd Is Driving the Future of Business.

Melden, A.I. (1955) Ethical theories. New York: Prentice-Hall.

Velasquez, M., Andre, C., Shanks, T., & Meyer, M. J. (2019). Thinking Ethically: A Framework for Moral Decision Making. Boston: Pearson. (CHAPTER 8)

AUTHOR DESCRIPTION

Introducing Astraea Bach, an esteemed author renowned for her critical thinking, reasoning, and problem-solving expertise. With an unwavering commitment to empowering individuals with essential skills, Astraea has established herself as a prominent figure in the field, dedicated to guiding readers through the complexities of the modern world.

Astraea's distinguished writing style captures the imagination, seamlessly intertwining intellectual depth with captivating storytelling. Through her eloquent prose, she adeptly conveys complex concepts, immersing readers in thought-provoking narratives that inspire profound introspection and foster a heightened intellectual curiosity.

With an extensive academic background and a wealth of practical experience, Astraea masterfully combines scholarly insights with real-world applications, ensuring her work resonates with readers from various backgrounds. Her meticulous research, intellectual rigor, and unwavering commitment to excellence shine through on every page, offering readers a trusted resource to enhance their critical thinking abilities.

Astraea's passion for empowering individuals to cultivate their critical thinking skills is palpable in her writing. With unwavering enthusiasm, she encourages readers to embrace curiosity, challenge conventional wisdom, and develop a strategic mindset to surmount obstacles and make well-informed decisions in an ever-evolving world.

Within the pages of her book, Astraea offers readers a transformative intellectual journey, guiding them through an immersive experience of discovery and growth. Her profound insights and practical strategies equip readers with the tools to navigate complex challenges, unlock their full potential, and embrace a future of limitless possibilities.

Prepare to embark on a captivating literary odyssey where Astraea Bach's critical thinking and problem-solving expertise will enlighten, inspire, and empower readers to embrace their intellectual prowess. Immerse yourself in the transformative power of Astraea's writing and embark on a path of intellectual enlightenment that will leave an indelible impact on your personal and professional life.